Workbook

D1404892

Your 10-Day Spiritual Action Plan for

Building Relationships That Last

KENNETH
COPELAND
PUBLICATIONS

by Kenneth and Gloria
Copeland

Includes material from the *Believer's Voice of Victory* magazine, *One Word From God Can Change Your Relationships, Living Contact, Honor—Walking in Honesty, Truth and Integrity, Be a Vessel of Honor, Hidden Treasures, How to Conquer Strife, One Word From God Can Change Your Formula for Success, Raising Children Without Fear, One Word From God Can Change Your Family, Hearing From Heaven,* Kenneth Copeland's Partner Letters, as well as newly created content and interactive action plans inspired by these resources.

Your 10-Day Spiritual Action Plan for Building Relationships That Last CD:

"I Will," Christen McCarley & Scott Allen © 2005 BubLand Music (BMI) • "Love That Never Changes," Michael Howell & Sherrie Howell © 2010 Dive Deep Music (ASCAP) • "Steal Away," Rachel Jackson © 2005 Kel-Jon Music (ASCAP) • "Holy Are You, God," Eric Hollar © 2005 Kel-Jon Music (ASCAP) • "Unto You," Scott Allen © 2004 Joel's Promise (BMI) • It's All About Love," Scott Allen & Robert Wirtz © 2005 Joel's Promise (BMI) • "God Is My Light," Scott Allen © 2005 Joel's Promise (BMI) • "Where I Belong," Scott Allen © 2005 Joel's Promise (BMI) • "I Can Hear Your Voice," Michael Howell © 1998 Heircraft Music Inc. (ASCAP) • "The Body of Christ," Scott Allen © 2005 Joel's Promise (BMI)

Your 10-Day Spiritual Action Plan for Building Relationships That Last

ISBN 978-1-60463-062-6   30-3020

15 14 13 12 11 10   6 5 4 3 2 1

© 2010 Eagle Mountain International Church Inc. aka Kenneth Copeland Ministries

For more information about Kenneth Copeland Ministries, call 800-600-7395 or visit www.kcm.org.

Table of Contents

How to Use
Your LifeLine Kit

How to Use
Your LifeLine Kit

We believe this *10-Day Spiritual Action Plan for Building Relationships That Last* will give you the tools you need to build strong, rewarding, godly relationships—the kind of relationships so many believers long for, but struggle to maintain.

God created us as social beings, made to encourage and strengthen one another in all we do (1 Thessalonians 5:11). It's our prayer that your marriage, children, family, friends, church fellowship and workplace relationships experience the highest integrity and rewards you could hope for or imagine. To accomplish this, we've created one of the most in-depth resources Kenneth Copeland Ministries has ever made available on this subject—all in one place. Here are some practical tips to get you started and help you make the most of this kit:

- Commit to making the next 10 days *your* days for renewing your mind. Set aside any distractions and be prepared to make adjustments in your life so you can get the most out of this kit.

- This plan should be a blessing, not a burden. If you miss a day or can't quite get through one day's materials, just start where you left off at your next opportunity. If you have to, be flexible with the kit to ensure you make it to the end. If you only have half an hour a day, that's fine—commit that! It may take longer to complete the kit, but you can be confident those 30 days will still be some of the most life-changing days you've ever had.

- Use this LifeLine workbook as your starting point each day, to guide your reading, listening, watching and journaling. Before you know it, you'll be saturating your life with God's Word like never before.

- We recommend that you:

  > **Read and journal** in the morning
  > **Meditate** on the scriptures daily
  > **Use** the CD and DVD products daily
  > as instructed in each chapter
  > **Read and journal** again at night

- Remember, the goal is to do a little every day. Steady doses are the best medicine.

- This is an action book! Have a pen handy to underline and take notes.

- Fully engage with all the materials. Write in your workbook, speak the scriptures, pray the prayers, sing with the music and take time to enjoy the materials in every way.

- Carry your daily action card and refer to it throughout your day as a connecting point with God.

- Make your study time focused. Do your best to remove distractions and find a quiet place.

You're closer than ever to *Building Relationships*—strong, rewarding, godly relationships—*That Last.* God loves you and He is *for* you. We're standing with you, and remember that "Jesus Is Lord!"

Chapter One
Your Most Important Relationship

My Father and My Friend
by Kenneth Copeland

In a book about building relationships that last, there's no better place to start than with the most important relationship of all: your relationship with the Lord. If that's not in order, all your other relationships will be out of order, too (Matthew 6:33).

So ask yourself: How much time do I spend fellowshiping with my heavenly Father? For most people, that's an embarrassing question. They get nervous at the very suggestion that a mere human being could actually fellowship with God. But they shouldn't. In fact, if they were getting their information from the Bible, living and talking and acting like who the Bible says they are in Jesus, they'd be living as though Jesus were their very best friend.

Of course, if they did that, some folks would think they'd gone off the deep end. I know because they already think that of me. They say, "Kenneth Copeland, you're out of your mind. You're trying to bring God down to your own level."

But what they don't realize is this: I didn't have one thing to do with that! He came down to our level of His own free will. He died and bore our sins by His own desire. I didn't have to bring Him down to my level. He came of His own accord.

I've had other people tell me, "You're trying to raise yourself up to be equal with God." But I didn't have anything to do with that either. The Bible says, "[He] hath raised us up together, and made us sit together in heavenly places" (Ephesians 2:6). I didn't do it. *He* did it! That's the good news! That's the gospel! I didn't have to lift myself up. He's already done it.

On top of all that, God Himself has said in His Word that He wants to get into a close relationship with us. First Corinthians 1:9 says He's called us into fellowship with Him!

A High Honor

Fellowship. We've been invited to fellowship with the Most High God, His Son,

Jesus, and the Holy Spirit. That's the highest honor that could ever be conferred on us!

Take a moment to get hold of that. You weren't just called to escape hell by the skin of your teeth. You weren't just called to be a church member. You weren't just called to be healed and prosperous. All those things are glorious, but that's not all He's called you to.

You're called to fellowship with Him, to walk with Him, talk with Him and discuss the things of life with Him. In fact, 2 Peter 1:4 says we're called to "participate in the divine nature" *(New International Version).*

Listen to me. Every believer, I don't care who you are, has the right to hear the voice of the Spirit of the living God. And not shouting at you from off in heaven somewhere, but from right there inside you.

I hear people say, "Well, God's never said anything to me." That's where they're wrong. He's been talking to all of us. He's sent His Spirit to lead us into the truth, and He's been doing His job just fine. The problem is, we haven't spent enough time fellowshiping with Him and listening to Him to hear what He's saying.

We've thought we were fellowshiping with Him, but most of the time, all we were really doing was having a string of emergency meetings—waiting until a crisis developed and then running to God for an answer.

I used to do that myself. But one time God said to me, *Kenneth, do you realize how much it would mean to Me for you to just come to Me sometimes and say, "Father, I didn't really come today to get anything. I've prayed about my needs already and Your Word says they're met according to Your riches in glory by Christ Jesus. So I just came to be with You. If you have anything You'd like to tell me, I'm ready to listen—and I want You to know that whatever I see in Your Word, I'll do it. I'll put it into effect in my life."*

Most people don't know much about that kind of relationship with God. But the

Apostle John calls that fellowship, and he says that kind of relationship with God is what gives us joy (see 1 John 1:3-4).

Emergency praying may give you relief. But fellowship—the intimacy of everyday closeness—is what gives you joy. You see, fellowship is not just relationship. It's beyond that. You can have a relationship without fellowship, but it's like having a marriage without love. The basic structure is there, but the heart of it is missing.

Crying "Abba"

Jesus had more than a relationship with God. They shared the same heart. In Mark 14, there's a gripping picture of the two of them in the Garden of Gethsemane, just a few hours before Calvary.

It shows Jesus falling on the ground and praying that if it were possible, the hour ahead might pass from Him. He knows He's about to bear the sin and grief of the whole world. He knows He will be alone, separated from His Father, and He's falling on His face before Him crying out, "Abba." "Daddy, Daddy." It was a very intimate moment.

But here's the amazing thing. According to the Bible, you and I can have that same kind of intimacy with God! In Romans 8:15-16, the Apostle Paul, speaking to believers, says, "For ye have not received the spirit of bondage again to fear; but ye have received the Spirit of adoption, whereby we cry, Abba, Father. The Spirit itself beareth witness with our spirit, that we are the children of God."

Do you hear what I'm telling you? The very same Spirit with which Jesus cried, "Daddy," is the same Spirit with which *you* cry out to God, "Daddy"!

If you've made Jesus Christ Lord of your life, Jesus is inside you. He's washed you clean by His blood so that now you, too, can cry, "Abba...Daddy"!

I wish I could just pop your head open and stuff this in there until your head and spirit were overflowing with it. God is just as much your Daddy as He is Jesus' Daddy. You have every ounce as much right to call Him Father as Jesus does because you belong to Jesus.

When I get to thinking about this, I get so excited about it. It's so thrilling to relax in God's presence! Being able to relax in His presence doesn't mean you lose your reverence for Him. In fact, you'll find that as you get to know Him more intimately, your reverence for Him will increase. But instead of being the kind of "reverence" that makes you dodge Him, it will be the kind of reverence that draws you to Him.

The Bottom Line

Here's the bottom line: You'll never truly know God's will and way for you—you'll never know Him for who He really is—until you learn to fellowship with Him, developing a good friendship with Him, and blessing Him with your friendship.

So begin right now. Make the decision that you will be one of those people they call a "Word person." I mean you will put God's Word as first place and final authority in your life.

No matter what the world says, no matter what practicality says, no matter what your feelings say—you will walk with God and make your friendship with Him the most important thing in your life.

That's when things will change for you. That's when you'll begin to discover that you really like your heavenly Father and that you can relax in His presence. That's when you'll begin to see all your other relationships fall into order.

Morning Reflection

How much time do you spend fellowshiping with the Father?

_____

_____

_____

_____

_____

_____

What is something God has recently said to you?

_____
_____
_____
_____
_____
_____

What can you do to make sure fellowship with the Lord is top priority in your life?

_____
_____
_____
_____
_____
_____

Today's
Connection Points

- **_Building Relationships That Last_ CD: "I Will" (Track 1)**

  Focus on Track 1 as you spend time fellowshiping with your heavenly Father.

- **DVD: "Your Most Important Relationship" (Chapter 1)**

  Make the decision to get your relationship with God in order, so all your other relationships will be in order, too.

- **_Love Confessions_ CD (Track 1)**

  Introduction, Deuteronomy 4:7; Psalms 23, 27:1, 46:10; Isaiah 41:10, 13

Faith
in Action

God wants you to know Him!
Commit to taking time each day to fellowship with Him.

Notes:

_____
_____
_____
_____
_____

Living Contact With God
by Gloria Copeland

Have you ever wished you had a strong, caring friend to help you, one who would join his strength with yours, making up the difference where you are weak? Well, I have good news. *God is that friend.* He has the strength you need, and He is looking for an opportunity to be a vital part of your daily life.

The Bible says, "The eyes of the Lord run to and fro throughout the whole earth, to show himself strong in the behalf of them whose heart is perfect toward him" (2 Chronicles 16:9). The word translated *perfect* there doesn't mean without a flaw. It simply means "faithful, loyal, dedicated and devoted."

So eager is God to find that person to whom He can show Himself strong that He will pass over a million people to find that one who is loyal to Him. He scans the earth looking for a person who will put Him first and let Him be God in his life.

For 4,000 years mankind was locked out of the presence of God by sin. But when Jesus went to the cross, all that changed. Jesus' sacrifice restored man's lost fellowship with God. Now as born-again believers, we "have full freedom and confidence to enter into the [Holy of] Holies [by the power and virtue] in the blood of Jesus" (Hebrews 10:19, *The Amplified Bible).* In effect, God has thrown open to us the door of fellowship.

Think of what that means. The Creator and Ruler of the entire universe has made Himself available to meet personally with you every day. You can commune with Him any time of the day or night.

"I'm here for you," He is saying. "Just draw near to Me and I'll draw near to you. I'll give you the wisdom you need. I'll strengthen and equip you and help you in every area of your life."

Living Contact

Although He has the solution for every problem, He won't chase you down to get your attention so He can give you those solutions. No, He will wait for you to do your part. What is your part? To draw near to Him. If you'll do that, He'll draw near to you in return. He gave us His Word on it (James 4:8).

The moment you turn to Him, He'll be there for you. But don't wait until hard times come to turn to Him. Develop a lifestyle of living contact.

Making living contact with God is simply fellowshiping with Him. It's talking to Him and listening to Him. It's setting aside the distractions and demands of life and taking time to commune with Him in His Word and in prayer. It's having fellowship with the Lord daily when things are going well so that when trouble comes, you'll be spiritually strong enough to overcome.

Jesus said in the world we will have tribulation (John 16:33). It doesn't matter who we are or how rich or well-educated, or even how much faith we have. In this life we will face some tests and trials. The difference is that when a Bible-believing, Spirit-filled child of God faces trouble, he doesn't face it alone. God says, "I will be with him in trouble; I will deliver him, and honour him" (Psalm 91:15). That's important. In time of trouble, *who* is with you makes a big difference. If your only help is your own natural strength and resources, you might come out of that trouble all right...and you might not. But when you're in union with God, you can be sure you'll come through just fine.

One of the best pictures of that union is what we see when wood strips are laminated together for strength. Just as the beams in a house are made stronger by laminating several layers of wood together, your ultimate strength comes from living in vital contact with God—abiding in the Vine. No longer are you dependent on *your* strength alone. You are laminated to Almighty God!

Keep the Union

First Corinthians 6:17 says, "The person

who is united to the Lord becomes one spirit with Him" *(The Amplified Bible).* The word *united* used there (or *joined* in the *King James Version)* means "laminated." It refers to something glued so tightly together that it becomes like one substance.

As we begin to spend time with the Lord, we begin to think like He thinks. We begin to act like He acts. We begin to hear from heaven moment by moment so that we can walk out the perfect will of God for our lives every day.

Once we understand the divine power that comes to us as we abide in Jesus, it is easy to see that if we want to live a victorious life—including strong relationships—we must first and foremost maintain our union and communion with Him. That is without question our most important responsibility.

If we'll maintain that union, He'll take care of everything else.

Unfortunately, however, many Christians do just the opposite. They become so busy maintaining the other things in their lives that they don't have time to spend with God. They spend their lives maintaining their houses and their lawns, their cars and their jobs. They even find time to maintain their hair and their fingernails. Yet they neglect the one thing that is vital to their life and well-being. They neglect their union with God.

Often they don't even realize it. They think that because they love the Lord and believe His Word, their union with Him is intact. But that's not necessarily so.

To be in union means to be joined together with something or someone. It's the act or instance of joining two or more things into one. Romans 7:4 likens our union with God to marriage. It says we've been married to Him.

Our goal is to become so in tune with Him that when He tells us to do something, we hear Him and obey. We should aim to be so closely joined to Him that the desires of our hearts, the thoughts of our minds, the words of our mouths and our every action become a reflection of the One with whom we are united.

That is God's desire, too. If He is to carry out His will in the earth, He must have people who will join themselves with Him in that way.

Perfect Union = Perfect Peace

How do you keep your mind stayed on God? By giving Him your attention. By putting His Word first place every day and focusing on it until it is the biggest thing in your life. *The Living Bible* says it this way: "Since you became alive again, so to speak, when Christ arose from the dead, now set your sights on the rich treasures and joys of heaven where he sits beside God in the place of honor and power. Let heaven fill your thoughts..." (Colossians 3:1-2).

Spiritually speaking, when you received Jesus as your Lord, you died to this world and became alive to God. So you should have as little desire for this world as a dead person does!

You don't have to spend your time worrying about worldly concerns. Instead, spend your time listening to what God has to say and keep your mind focused on Him. Isaiah 26:3 says, "Thou [God] wilt keep him in perfect peace, whose mind is stayed on thee...." Jesus confirmed that when He said, "Peace I leave with you, my peace I give unto you: not as the world giveth, give I unto you. Let not your heart be troubled, neither let it be afraid" (John 14:27).

If you keep your mind on the world and stay in union with it, you won't have any peace. That's because the world doesn't have any peace. If you give the majority of your time and attention to worldly matters and secular entertainment, you will be carnally minded, and the Bible says, "To be carnally minded is death; but to be spiritually minded is life and peace" (Romans 8:6).

In other words, if you think like the world thinks, you'll receive the same results the world does. And instead of enjoying rich, godly relationships, you'll suffer with the paper-thin facades of the world. Instead of laying hold of heavenly prosperity and healing, the depression, sickness and poverty of the world will lay hold of you! You won't be full of good news, you'll be full of bad news. Trying to build relationships solely based on the popular thinking of this world will always result in failure.

You're Connected

When someone has friends in high places, we sometimes say, "He's connected." Well if you're maintaining living contact with God, you're connected! You're connected with the highest ruler and authority in existence. You have a connection with the power above every other power, and you need to maintain an awareness of that connection. You ought to think about it all through the day.

If you'll do that, then the faith and power of God will rise up within you to deal with whatever comes your way in life, or in any relationship. When you are joined, or laminated, to God, that living connection will make all the difference. Instead of depending on yourself, you can truly say, "I can do all things through *Christ* which strengtheneth me" (Philippians 4:13)!

Evening Reflection

What does it mean to have living contact with God?

_____

_____

_____

_____

What changed in terms of man's relationship with the Lord when Jesus went to the cross?

_____

_____

_____

_____

What distractions has the devil used to try and sever your living connection with the Lord?

_____

_____

_____

_____

Notes:

_____

_____

_____

_____

_____

_____

_____

_____

_____

_____

_____

_____

_____

_____

_____

_____

_____

_____

_____

_____

Today's
Prayer of Faith

Father God, more than anything else, I want to know You. I want to spend time with You, share my life and be in constant fellowship with You. As I commit my time to You, thank You for revealing Your love to me more each day. In Jesus' Name. Amen.

Real-Life Testimonies
to Help Build Your Faith

Receiving the Father's Love

I want to thank you, Brother Copeland, for teaching on love. I have been watching you and Keith Moore on the broadcast. When you spoke of receiving the Father's love, it was a new concept to me. I was born and raised in church, but I just never got it.

I have endured much in my life and struggled in relationships. But I never knew the problem was that I could not accept love. When you prayed that love would flow through us, I suddenly understood what has been missing— *love!* I am free now!

As Keith Moore prayed, I could see the love in his eyes. That's it! That's what I have been missing and always desired from God, myself and others—love. What a blessing! Thank you from the bottom of my heart.

J.D.
Michigan

Chapter Two
Love Above All

Grow Up in Love

by Gloria Copeland

In Mark 12:29-31, Jesus states, "The most important [commandment] is this: 'Hear, O Israel, the Lord our God, the Lord is one. Love the Lord your God with all your heart and with all your soul and with all your mind and with all your strength.' The second is this: 'Love your neighbor as yourself.' There is no commandment greater than these" *(New International Version)*. Studying love is clearly the focal point for studying anything at all to do with relationships—whether it's with the Lord or with others.

Some people think love is so basic, it's something only spiritual beginners must study. They consider the gifts of the Spirit—like tongues and interpretation, the gifts of healings and miracles—as more relevant to the mature believer. But the gifts of the Spirit are not marks of spiritual maturity. The Corinthian church abounded in those gifts, yet the Apostle Paul referred to them as "mere infants...in Christ... still [unspiritual, having the nature] of the flesh" (1 Corinthians 3:1, 3, *The Amplified Bible*).

As wonderful as the gifts of the Spirit are, the Bible teaches that it's the fruit of the spirit— "love, joy, peace, longsuffering, gentleness, goodness, faith, meekness, [and] temperance" (Galatians 5:22-23)—that indicate a person is walking in the spirit and not the flesh.

If you want to know whether you're a spiritual person or not, look to see if you are walking in love. You simply can't walk in the spirit or be a spiritual person without being ruled by love. The reason I single out love is because it is the foundation upon which all the other fruit rest. The others flow out of love.

To find out just how important love is in the economy of God, read the first few verses of 1 Corinthians 13:

> If I speak in the tongues of men and of angels, but have not love, I am only a resounding gong or a clanging cymbal. If I have the gift of prophecy and can fathom all mysteries and can fathom all knowledge, and if I have a faith that can move mountains, but have not love, I am nothing. If I give all I possess to the poor and surrender my body to the flames, but have not love, I gain nothing (verses 1-3, *New International Version*).

Love is the bottom line. Nothing counts without it. In short, you and I can't go anywhere spiritually or anywhere with our relationships until we get our love walk straight!

No wonder the Bible tells us to: "Eagerly pursue and seek to acquire [this] love [make it your aim, your great quest]" (1 Corinthians 14:1, *The Amplified Bible*). Living a life ruled by the love of God is what opens us up to walk in the spirit and live in the highest measure of the blessing and power of God!

That's why Paul prayed that we would be able to know and experience "the love of Christ." Because then we will be able to obtain "the richest measure of the divine Presence, and become a body wholly filled and flooded with God Himself" (Ephesians 3:19, *The Amplified Bible*).

Our Only Law

Under the new covenant, love is our only law. Jesus said, "This is my commandment, That ye love one another, as I have loved you" (John 15:12). Romans 13:10 says, "Love is the fulfilling of the law."

What's more, when we were born again, God put His own loving nature inside us. Now "the love of God is shed abroad in our hearts by the Holy Ghost which is given unto us" (Romans 5:5).

If you're a Christian, love is your supernatural, natural disposition. But it will not simply take over your life without your cooperation. If you want to walk in love, you'll have to make a decision to yield to that force of love on the inside of you. You'll have to resist the selfish tendencies of the flesh and choose to live a life governed by love.

Of course, when I say "love" here, I'm not talking about the emotional counterfeit the world calls love. That kind of love is dependent on circumstances and feelings.

God's love isn't like that. It's constant. It's unconditional. The chief ingredient of the God kind of love is self-sacrifice for the benefit of the one loved. It continues to love people whether or not it receives a response. Divine love is not self-seeking. It is self-giving.

God doesn't just love the lovely. He loves the unlovely, too. No matter how bad or mean someone might be, if they'll turn to Him, He'll cleanse them and forgive them.

That's the way God loves us, and that's the way He expects us to love each other. In 1 Corinthians 13, He gives us a detailed description of that kind of love.

> Love endures long and is patient and kind; love never is envious nor boils over with jealousy, is not boastful or vainglorious, does not display itself haughtily. It is not conceited (arrogant and inflated with pride); it is not rude (unmannerly) and does not act unbecomingly. Love (God's love in us) does not insist on its own rights or its own way, for it is not self-seeking; it is not touchy or fretful or resentful; it takes no account of the evil done to it [it pays no attention to a suffered wrong]. It does not rejoice at injustice and unrighteousness, but rejoices when right and truth prevail. Love bears up under anything and everything that comes, is ever ready to believe the best of every person, its hopes are fadeless under all circumstances, and it endures everything [without weakening]. Love never fails... (verses 4-8, *The Amplified Bible*).

That kind of love is the distinguishing mark of a Christian. We're called to live a life of love just like Jesus did.

Walking in love means we lay down our own selfish tendencies and desires. We set aside our feelings and behave kindly and gently to those around us, regardless of how they act. We don't have to be concerned about looking out for our rights, because when we walk in love, God takes care of us.

Develop Your Love Walk

Making these changes is not as difficult as it may sound. In fact, the key to developing your love walk is wonderfully simple. You do it by maintaining living contact with God just as we talked about in the last session—fellowshiping with Him in the Word and in prayer, staying in union and communion with Him, and letting His life flow through you.

Remember, Jesus Himself taught us the principle of sustained communion. He said:

> Just as no branch can bear fruit of itself without abiding in (being vitally united to) the vine, neither can you bear fruit unless you abide in Me. I am the Vine; you are the branches. Whoever lives in Me and I in him bears much (abundant) fruit. However, apart from Me [cut off from vital union with Me] you can do nothing (John 15:4-5, *The Amplified Bible*).

First John 4:16-17 says it this way: "God is love, and he who dwells and continues in love dwells and continues in God, and God dwells and continues in him. In this [union and communion with Him] love is brought to completion and attains perfection with us...because as He is, so are we in this world" *(The Amplified Bible)*.

The Apostle Paul prayed "that [we might arrive] at really mature manhood (the completeness of personality which is nothing less than the standard height of Christ's own perfection)" and that, *"Enfolded in love,* let us grow up in every way and in all things into Him Who is the Head, [even] Christ..." (Ephesians 4:13, 15, *The Amplified Bible*). I've come to realize that love is the single, most important key to growing up in God and in our relationships with others. In fact, if we don't grow up in love...we won't grow up at all!

Morning Reflection

How would you explain the biblical definition of love?

_____

_____

_____

_____

_____

How is the biblical definition of love different from the world's definition?

_____

_____

_____

_____

_____

How is walking in love related to your spiritual life?

_____

_____

_____

_____

_____

_____

_____

Today's Connection Points

- **Building Relationships That Last CD: "Love That Never Changes" (Track 2)**

  Meditate on how much God loves you as you listen to this track today.

- **DVD: "Believe the Love" (Chapter 2)**

  Believe, develop and exercise your faith in the fullness of God's love.

- **Love Confessions CD (Track 2)**

  Mark 11:22-23; John 3:16; 1 Corinthians 13:1-8; Ephesians 3:14-21;
  1 John 4:18 _(The Amplified Bible);_ 1 John 5:18

Faith in Action

As you interact with others today, examine your heart to see if you're walking in love—and ask yourself what you can do to practice the love of Christ that's in you.

Notes:

_____

_____

_____

_____

_____

_____

_____

_____

_____

_____

_____

_____

_____

_____

_____

_____

_____

_____

_____

_____

_____

_____

_____

_____

_____

_____

_____

_____

_____

_____

_____

_____

_____

_____

_____

_____

_____

_____

Becoming the Image of Love

by Kenneth Copeland

As born-again children of God, you and I ought to be growing up into the image of Jesus. With every day that passes, we should be walking, talking, thinking and acting more like Him.

I realize that thought shocks religious folks. They think it's practically blasphemy for us to imagine we could ever be like the Lord. But the fact is, the New Testament plainly states that is our destiny.

Jesus Himself said, "He that believeth on me, the works that I do shall he do also; and greater works than these shall he do; because I go unto my Father" (John 14:12).

The Apostle Paul wrote that we are predestined "to be conformed to the image of [God's] Son, that he might be the firstborn among many brethren" (Romans 8:29) and to "grow up into him in all things, which is the head, even Christ" (Ephesians 4:15).

The Apostle John said it this way: "As he is, so are we in this world" (1 John 4:17).

As amazing as those scriptures are, many believers instinctively know they're true and instantly bear witness that they've been born again to be just like Jesus.

God wants to do the same things through us that He did through Him!

Some of us have stepped into that on occasion. We've had moments when we experienced the life and power of God flowing through us. But we haven't yet lived in that place on a day-to-day basis.

From Our Heads to Our Hearts

Why haven't we? What is it that we've been missing?

The fullness of God's love.

We've done well in developing our awareness of the fact that God resides on the inside of us. We've come to understand that we've been born of God's Spirit and His Word. But recently the Lord told me we need a much higher degree of revelation that God is love, and that His love is in us *to be used.* We must purposely develop and exercise our faith in His love.

One effective way to begin developing faith in God's love for you is by reading through the Bible and substituting the word *Love* for the word *God.* That's a perfectly scriptural thing to do because the Bible doesn't just say that God *has* love. It says He *is* Love.

So you can say when you read Psalm 23, for instance, "Love is my Shepherd. I shall not want…. Even though I walk through the valley of the shadow of death, I fear no evil because Love is with me. Love prepares a table for me in the presence of my enemies…."

If you'll meditate the Word that way for a while, you'll come to the point where you can't think of God without thinking of love. The two will absolutely become so united in your mind that the very thought God might not love you will seem preposterous. How could God not love you? He *is* Love!

With that fact settled, you can develop your faith further by acknowledging just how great God's love for you truly is. You can spend time meditating on the fact that God loves you just as much as He loves Jesus.

"Whoa…! I'm not sure I can believe that," you might say.

You can if you believe the words of Jesus because He's the One who said it. When He was praying for us as His disciples in John 17:23, He said to the Father, "…thou hast sent me, and hast loved them, as thou hast loved me."

What's more, three verses later Jesus told us that same love has been put in our hearts. That's right! He said, "I have declared unto them thy name, and will declare it: that the love wherewith thou hast loved me may be in them, and I in them" (verse 26). Romans 5:5 confirms that truth by telling us that "the love of God is shed abroad in our hearts by the Holy Ghost which is given unto us."

Think about that! God not only loves you just as powerfully as He loves Jesus, He has put that same mighty love inside of you so that you can love like He loves! I know that's staggering to your human mind but dare to believe it anyway. Receive it as truth in your heart. Lift your hands and say, "Father, I believe You love me just as much as You love Jesus. I believe that very love is in me now. I accept the commandment to use that love and I believe fear will be driven out of me as I do!"

Practice His Presence

Since faith without works is dead, if you truly believe those words, you'll not only say them you'll also put them into action. You'll start practicing the life of love. One way to do that is by practicing God's presence in your daily life. Develop an awareness that Love is constantly with you by talking to Him all the time.

First thing in the morning when you open your eyes say, "Good morning, Lord. I love You and praise You today. I'm so glad You never leave me nor forsake me. I receive Your love for me and I want You to know my desire is to be a blessing to You. Help me, teach me and train me—whatever You desire for me to do, I'll be willing and obedient. I'll do it with a happy heart."

When you start to practice God's presence like that, it will change how you act throughout the day. You'll start being more loving and kind—even when other people aren't around to notice—because you'll know the Lord is there and you have no desire to grieve Him. If your car won't start, for example, you won't be so prone to get angry, slap the steering wheel and spout some kind of Christianized profanity at it, such as "Dad-Gummit!" The spirit behind that kind of reaction is the same one behind swearing.

It's destructive to act that way even when you aren't directing your anger toward other people because it's a form of practicing bad temper. If you practice anger and ill temper, they will stay on the surface and activate before you have the opportunity to stop them. Don't express anger even against material objects. Instead take authority over that anger and say, "No, you don't. I'm not yielding to you. You get back under control right now."

That will be easy to do when you're practicing God's presence because you know He is lovely, kind and gentle; and you will not want to offend Him by displaying an ugly attitude toward anything at any time. Granted, you won't be able to make all the changes you want to make in the first hour and a half. It takes time to do this. But you can make the decision in the next moment and a half and then walk it out moment by moment.

As you do, be quick to judge yourself. (Notice I didn't say *condemn yourself,* I said *judge yourself.*) When you step out of love, stop right then and say, "Forgive me, Lord. That was unloving. I repent of that and receive Your forgiveness and cleansing right now. Thank You for helping me be like You."

If the devil tries to bring that sin to your mind again later, resist him. Say, "No, that's been cleansed by the blood of Jesus. It doesn't even exist anymore." Then switch your mental gears and put your mind on Jesus. Purposely meditate on how wonderfully loving He is and remind yourself that His loving nature is in you.

Practice Makes Perfect

What does this have to do with building lasting relationships with others? Well, to complete this process of developing your faith in God's love, you must not only allow it to flow to you but *through* you to others. As 1 John 4:12 says, "If we love one another, God dwelleth in us, and His love is perfected in us."

Remember the old saying *practice makes perfect?* That's absolutely the truth. The way to perfect God's love in you is by practicing that love toward other people.

Don't just practice it on the easy ones, either. Don't just focus on loving the people who are kind and gracious to you. (The Bible says even rank sinners can do that.) Determine to love those who irritate you and act ugly toward you. Purposely love those who have hurt you.

Start by making sure you have forgiven them of any wrong they have done to you. Even if you don't emotionally feel like forgiving them, do it anyway by faith. Say, "Father, I am forgiving this person out of obedience to Your Word. I refuse to hold anything against them. Right now by faith I receive from You the grace to love them." Then pray for that person. Ask God to help them and bless them.

Don't sit around waiting for some kind of supernatural warm, fuzzy feeling to make you do it, either. Just pray for them by an act of your will. Ask God to help you see that person the way He sees them.

Faith without action is dead so take the time in prayer to "see" them the way God does. Start by picturing them in your mind and then visualize Jesus coming right up behind them and taking them in His arms. See them totally engulfed in Him. Then think *Yes, Lord, that's the way You treated me. You loved me and had mercy on me when I didn't deserve it. Help me do for them what You did for me. Lord, I let Your forgiveness and compassion for them find expression through me.*

You may think you can't do that right now. But I guarantee if you'll step out in faith, you'll tap in to the love of God and find out you can. You'll find that the more you believe the love God has for you and the more you practice it toward others, the more it is perfected in you.

As you keep on developing that love, with every day that passes, you'll grow up a little more into the image of Jesus. You'll start walking, talking, thinking and acting more like Him. The works Jesus did, you will boldly do also…and your relationships will blossom as others see *Him* in you.

Evening Reflection

What kind of love does the Word say God has put in your heart?

_____
_____
_____
_____

What part does meditation play in walking in love?

_____
_____
_____
_____

How do you "practice love"?

_____
_____
_____
_____

Notes:

_____
_____
_____
_____
_____
_____
_____
_____
_____
_____
_____
_____
_____
_____
_____
_____

Today's Prayer of Faith

Father, You are Love and You have put Your love in my heart. Help me to practice love today in all I do and say, so others may see You in me. In Jesus' Name. Amen.

Real-Life Testimonies
to Help Build Your Faith

The Power of Love

I have suffered from obsessive-compulsive, fear-filled thoughts for many years. But the outward manifestation of the power of God in the aftermath of 9/11 made an impression on me and I began to pray and seek God. I didn't know the term "born again" but I knew I was different somehow.

One night I saw Kenneth on *Larry King Live* with Pat Boone and it encouraged me, so I tuned in to your TV program. I haven't missed a program since! It is good to see a real tough guy like Brother Copeland talk about God's love. It made me see that love is not just some weak, sentimental thing, but a force of immense power. I cannot get enough of the Word of God in my life now!

A.W.
New Jersey

Chapter Three
The Power of Forgiveness

The Happy Marriage Formula

by Gloria Copeland

God desires for your life and marriage to be like days of heaven on earth. And that is possible...when you do things God's way and obey His commands.

I know it's possible because Ken and I have been married nearly 50 years, and we have never been happier! The longer we live together, the better it gets because we have come into agreement about the way we live our lives. The result is truly days of heaven on earth.

Ken and I desire for you to have that, too. We desire for you to have a happy, blessed home and family. We want to encourage you to know that it is possible when you apply the principles found in the Bible.

In the Word of God, there is what I consider to be a *happy marriage formula*. It's found in 1 Corinthians 13:5: "Love (God's love in us) does not insist on its own rights or its own way, for it is not self-seeking; it is not touchy or fretful or resentful; it takes no account of the evil done to it [it pays no attention to a suffered wrong]" *(The Amplified Bible)*.

Of course, as we saw last session, the entire chapter of 1 Corinthians 13 is our guidepost for walking in love. But this particular verse teaches us so many things. *It's perhaps the greatest marriage scripture I have ever found about walking in love*. Let's break it down.

"Love (God's love in us) does not insist on its own rights or its own way, for it is not self-seeking."

To begin with, to have a strong marriage, we must recognize that the love of God is not selfish. Have you ever noticed that selfish people are never happy? And here's why: They are always thinking about themselves instead of others. They are always striving to get their needs met and get what they want.

The Bible tells us it is in giving that we receive (Luke 6:38). Unselfish people walk in love and are always looking for ways to bless others (including their spouses). They are sowing love and they will reap love. These people will live in happiness, joy and peace.

"Love is not touchy or fretful or resentful."

When I first read 1 Corinthians 13 years ago and it became a revelation to me, I wrote verse 5 on little cards and put them up where I could see them. When I would want to get mad, I would say, "I walk in love. I'm not touchy, fretful or resentful." I did that over and over until I learned not to respond in anger. I did whatever it took to get these words working in my life!

Today they still help me stay on track. If I begin to get mad and yield to temper, I think about this scripture. My life is changed as a result.

Remember, you have to practice the love of God. Some people *practice anger.* They are mad at everyone and everything around them. Being angry has become a habit in their lives.

As born-again children of God, our habit should be to yield to the nature of the Spirit of God in us. His nature is love—we must decide to yield to that!

"Love takes no account of the evil done to it [it pays no attention to a suffered wrong]."

This is so important: *Love forgives.*

Love doesn't hold a grudge. If you desire to have a happy marriage, you must forgive one another.

Someone once said that refusing to forgive someone and expecting things to go well with you is like drinking poison and thinking the other person is going to die. It just doesn't work that way. Unforgiveness doesn't hurt the other person—*it hurts you.* When you forgive, however, you are set free.

Forgiving is a very significant part of love. We can be habitual forgivers because God has forgiven us of so much.

Even When It Isn't Easy

First Corinthians 13:13 in *The Amplified Bible* defines love as "true affection for God and man, growing out of God's love for and in us."

As we love God, we are able to love the people around us, even when it isn't easy.

It may be hard to believe, but in the early years of our marriage, Ken would occasionally do something I didn't like. I was learning to walk in love, so instead of becoming outwardly angry, I just wouldn't respond, even though I was really aggravated! But, I didn't forgive. By not responding I was just covering up my disobedience to the Word. But I knew the truth, and so did the Lord.

You see, walking in love is not a matter of just holding your tongue. It means not being touchy, fretful or resentful. It means paying no attention to a suffered wrong.

Love is a matter of what is in your heart.

I learned that. I discovered when I didn't respond in love I became my own worst enemy. No one comes out on top by staying in strife.

In marriage, it's vital for a husband and wife to walk in love and have respect for the other's opinions. Today, Ken and I are living proof it can be done. However, we would not be where we are in our marriage if both of us had not been determined to obey the Word where love is concerned.

Walking in love is our law. It is our command. We know we cannot please God unless we love everyone—including each other.

So if you find yourself being touchy, fretful or resentful, know that you're out of the will of God. It is as simple as that.

Choose to forgive and walk in love, and have a happy marriage!

Morning Reflection

How can selfishness hurt a marriage?

_____
_____
_____
_____
_____
_____
_____

How can you practice not being touchy, fretful or resentful?

_____
_____
_____
_____
_____
_____
_____

Why is forgiveness a significant part of love?

_____
_____
_____
_____
_____
_____

Today's Connection Points

- ● **Building Relationships That Last CD:
"Steal Away" (Track 3)**

  As you listen to this track today, "steal away" with God and focus on His perfect love.

- ● **DVD: "Live Free From Strife" (Chapter 3)**

  When you forgive, you not only free the other person but you free yourself from unforgiveness and strife.

- ● **Love Confessions CD (Track 3)**

  Deuteronomy 7:7-8, 10:14-15; Psalms 17:7, 26:3, 36:7, 40:10-11, 69:16, 91:14-16

Faith in Action

**Choose to walk in love today. Choose to not be selfish, touchy, fretful or resentful.**
Choose to walk in forgiveness—immediately!

Notes:

_____
_____
_____
_____
_____
_____
_____
_____
_____
_____
_____
_____
_____
_____
_____
_____
_____
_____
_____
_____
_____
_____
_____
_____

Forgive, Forget and Be Blessed

by Kenneth Copeland

Let's look closely at forgiveness, because living in forgiveness is crucial when it comes to building relationships. But did you know it is also crucial to the operation of your faith? In fact, we have the ability to operate with the highest form of faith just by following the outline Jesus has given us in the Word.

I want to share with you the power God has given to us when we walk in the light of forgiveness. We'll see clearly that there is a very close relationship between forgiveness and the love of God.

Mark 11:22-24 has got to be the most well-known scripture reference there is on the subject of faith. Jesus is teaching about the God kind of faith and how it operates. He says:

> Have faith in God. For verily I say unto you, That whosoever shall say unto this mountain, Be thou removed, and be thou cast into the sea; and shall not doubt in his heart, but shall believe that those things which he saith shall come to pass; he shall have whatsoever he saith. Therefore, I say unto you, What things soever ye desire, when ye pray, believe that ye receive them, and ye shall have them.

Let's read on. I want to focus attention on Jesus' words in verses 25-26: "And when ye stand praying, forgive, if ye have aught against any; that your Father also which is in heaven may forgive you your trespasses. But if ye do not forgive, neither will your Father which is in heaven forgive your trespasses."

Jesus makes the act of forgiveness an integral part of the faith life. In verse 26 He very plainly states a spiritual law: If you do not forgive, then your Father in heaven will not forgive you. This ties in closely with His teaching in Matthew 18 where He explains to His disciples about the power of agreement.

Matthew 18:19 says, "Again I say unto you, That if two of you shall agree on earth as touching any thing that they shall ask, it shall

be done for them of my Father which is in heaven."

The Amplified Bible says, "…if two of you on earth agree (harmonize together, make a symphony together)…."

Jesus places a tremendous importance on harmony and agreement between believers, and forgiveness plays a vital part in that harmony.

The 15-Cent Debt

When Peter asked Jesus how many times he should forgive his brother, Jesus answered, "Until seventy times seven." (That's 490 times!) Then He related a parable in Matthew 18:23-35. Get your Bible and read those verses now to get them fresh in your mind and spirit. Once you've read them, return to this teaching and we'll continue.

In these verses, we see that a servant owed his lord a debt equivalent to millions of dollars today. Though he is forgiven of that large debt, he refuses to forgive a fellow servant of only a 15-cent debt! When the Lord hears about it, He delivers that servant to the tormentors. Verse 32 says He called that servant a wicked servant. God looks at unforgiveness as wickedness.

This parable shows the consequences of walking in unforgiveness. The servant was forgiven of a large debt, but then would not release his fellow servant of a small, insignificant debt. His attitude of unforgiveness cost him much more than the debt he owed.

There can be no room in our lives for unforgiveness. When a believer is unwilling to forgive, he puts himself automatically in a position where Satan can torment and attack him. I want you to realize it was only a 15-cent debt that caused that servant to be tormented. It is the little 15-cent debts we tend to overlook. If someone does or says something to you that hurts, you usually try to shrug it off; but that is the kind of thing Satan will try to take advantage of. The little 15-cent debts we don't forgive are what give Satan place in our lives—the small things we do and say, the cutting words and unkind remarks.

Clogging the Pipeline

As I was praying about this, the Spirit of God showed me what happens when we allow unforgiveness to build up in our spirits. I saw a pipe stretching between God and me. The pipe was a funnel for the power of God. At God's end, the power was flooding in, but at my end, there was only a trickle coming out. Something was clogging the pipe somewhere along the way. The Spirit of God showed me that unforgiveness was stopping the flow of God's power. Those little 15-cent debts had been like silt—tiny bits of dirt and filth—that had built up a wall inside the pipe. When I recognized that, I quickly repented and allowed the Holy Spirit to purge my spirit of the unforgiveness and clean out the pipe so God's power could flow unhindered.

We are instructed to forgive one another even as God has forgiven us—freely, unconditionally. Gloria just showed you 1 Corinthians 13:5 where it says that love takes no account of the evil done to it—pays no attention to a suffered wrong.

The things people do or say to you can get close enough to hurt you only if you act outside of love yourself. If you resent and hold an offense against someone, it injures you. Unforgiveness, like strife, is a thief that cometh to steal, kill and destroy. It holds you in bondage and renders your prayer life powerless.

When you forgive, you not only free the other person but you also free yourself from unforgiveness and strife.

It's Time to Forgive

It is time for the Body of Christ to come to maturity in this area. We have studied much about how to operate proficiently in faith. Now we must operate just as proficiently in forgiveness and love.

What I am sharing with you is spiritual truth. It is totally contrary to the world's way of thinking and goes against the grain of human behavior. To live and walk in forgiveness, you will have to resist pride. At times, you will have to go to your brother and ask his forgiveness. You will have to forgive him, even though every ounce of your being wants to strike out against him. You will have to forgive others, even as God for Christ's sake has forgiven you. But remember, you cannot make it without God's forgiveness. You cannot have His forgiveness unless you forgive.

To cleanse your spirit of unforgiveness, simply:

- Confess the sin of unforgiveness according to 1 John 1:9.

- Forgive as an act of your will and obedience; not your feelings. Do it the same way you would receive healing or anything else by faith. Make a quality decision that you're going to do what God's Word instructs—no matter what.

- Speak and act in accordance with that decision. Refuse to say anything negative about that person. Refuse to rehearse in your mind or with your mouth the hurt that has been caused you. Instead, look for opportunities to bless that person both in word and in deed.

- Believe that you receive forgiveness and cleansing from all unrighteousness—including any remembrance of being wronged. You are forgiven even as He forgave. God's power is cleansing power. It will cleanse your consciousness completely.

- Praise God and give thanks that it is done.

It is so important to have a forgiving heart. In order for us as believers to effectively reach the world with the gospel—the good news of Jesus Christ—the power of God must be allowed to flow through us. We cannot be used much by the Holy Spirit when our spirits are clogged with bitterness and resentment and unforgiveness. This places a serious responsibility on our shoulders.

Only when we have forgiving hearts will true harmony come into our homes and bring us into a position of total harmony with God and with one another.

Make it your goal to develop and maintain an attitude of forgiveness. See that you keep your heart clean before God. Be quick to repent when you are faced with opportunities for strife. Don't allow Satan any place in your life. Keep the pipe clean and the power of God flowing!

Evening Reflection

How is forgiveness tied to faith?

_____
_____
_____
_____

How has unforgiveness "clogged your pipeline"?

_____
_____
_____
_____

What are the steps to forgiveness?

_____
_____
_____
_____

Notes:

_____
_____
_____
_____
_____
_____
_____
_____
_____
_____
_____
_____
_____
_____
_____
_____
_____
_____
_____
_____
_____

Today's Prayer of Faith

Father, in the Name of Jesus, I make a fresh commitment to You to live in peace and harmony—not only with my brothers and sisters in the Body of Christ, but with my friends, associates, neighbors and family. I let go of all bitterness, resentment, envying, strife and unkindness in any form. I give no place to the devil. I forgive. Amen!

Real-Life Testimonies
to Help Build Your Faith

Marriage Restored

I want to give all honor and glory to the Lord for returning my husband to me after we had been separated for 1½ years. Without the Lord's strength and comfort, I would not have stayed the course. He taught me patience, perseverance, wisdom and compassion. Ultimately, He has and does continue to teach me how to forgive others of their sins as He has forgiven mine.

S.H.
Qatar

Chapter Four
Becoming the Lord's Vessel

The Honorable Life
by Kenneth Copeland

Honor. The world defines it in many ways, but I define it as "a keen sense of ethical conduct." It is personal integrity. When we study the building blocks of lasting relationships, we must take time to study the importance of living a life of honor in all we do. We honor God by living life as He directs. God has promised that if we honor Him and act on His Word, He will honor us (1 Samuel 2:30).

Honesty and Honor Go Together

In 1 Peter 2:11-12, Peter stated, "Dearly beloved, I beseech you as strangers and pilgrims, abstain from fleshly lusts, which war against the soul; having your conversation honest among the Gentiles: that, whereas they speak against you as evildoers, they may by your good works, which they shall behold, glorify God in the day of visitation."

The word *honest* in that verse is closely related to the word *honor.* Peter is saying here, "Let your conversation—your manner of life— be honorable among the gentiles."

Among the Jews of Peter's day the word *gentile* was used to refer to nations or people without God. If you study the book of Ephesians, you will see that at one time you and I were gentiles, but now we who were afar off have been brought near to God by the blood of His Son, Jesus Christ (Ephesians 2:13).

This passage is talking about the way we should act toward those who don't know God. Our honorable manner of life, our living honestly among the gentiles, is important!

Let just one or two preachers get in trouble and suddenly all preachers have trouble because of the way a few "Christian" ministers have lived their lives and conducted their business. Instead of walking in honor before the gentiles, these few have disgraced and damaged all believers. We must learn to walk honestly before the gentiles, so they will behold our good works and glorify our heavenly Father.

No Discounts, Please!

One time a preacher came in to a convenience store where I was shopping. He was trying to talk the clerk into giving him a discount on his shotgun shells because he was a minister. It embarrassed me. It almost made me want to curse so that clerk wouldn't think I was a preacher, too.

I just stood there and shook my head.

The clerk behind the counter got really irritated at the man. He could not have given him a discount, even if he had wanted to, because he did not own the store.

I thought, *My goodness, I can guess what this guy is going to start saying about preachers.*

It doesn't have to be that way, and it shouldn't be that way. The first time I really saw how it should be was while I was a student at Oral Roberts University. Someone told me how Brother Roberts had responded when a barber offered him a discount on his haircut.

"No sir," said Brother Roberts. "I don't accept discounts just because I'm a preacher. I'm not a poor man."

He would not receive it.

"I'll pay the same price as anybody else," he told the barber. "If God puts it in your heart to invest a portion of your income as an offering in this ministry, or any other ministry, that's between you and Him; but I'll pay the full price for my own haircut."

That thrills me. It thrilled that barber, too. He hadn't had many preachers coming in and talking to him like that. Some of them would probably beg him out of his combs if he would give them away.

We are going to have to stop this begging business and dishonorable activity. It is a losing attitude for each of us ministers and for all believers. It is a bad representation of our Lord. Do you think Jesus would be begging people for a discount? No, no, a thousand times, no!

You never heard Jesus beg. You never

heard Him stand up and mock anyone, not even the government. To have biblical honor means to honor and obey the political authorities, even in the face of bad government and poor treatment. You cannot get much worse government and poorer treatment than what was coming out of Rome in Jesus' day.

You never heard Jesus criticize others behind their backs. If He had anything to say about others, He said it to them face to face. Because of that, the Bible says that many of the Jews and Pharisees followed Him. We tend to focus on the ones who opposed and rejected Him, but the Bible says that many of them did believe on Him and follow Him—in fact, great numbers of them did.

Honor Begets Honor

We must honor God by living life as He has directed—every day! This means honoring those above us, being subject to them.

If your superiors mistreat you, crying and moaning won't help. If you keep crying, "They don't like me," then they won't. There really is no reason for them to like you. They don't know God, and you are acting like you don't either.

You are a man or woman of honor. What do you do when someone cheats you out of your vacation or your overtime pay or your rightful promotion? You say: "Lord, You know what's happening here. I'm being treated unjustly. You know it, I know it, and they know it. I just turn this situation over to You. You handle it any way You want."

Then a strange thing will happen: In the end, you will come out ahead. How will that happen? By honoring God, then living in His honor and by your own honesty.

There is nothing that we can't accomplish in honor, in God's honor. There is no place we can't go, no goal we can't reach—if we keep an honorable attitude.

An Honorable Attitude

Christian people can be snobs, though. Some can even be so upright and uptight that they don't live honorably, even when they think they are.

I knew a woman in Pensacola, Florida, which is the home of a U.S. naval base with hundreds and hundreds of sailors. When one aircraft carrier docks there, 3,000 people or more may disembark and head to town. Most of the people there know when a carrier or some other large warship has docked.

This dear lady would take tracts with her name and phone number on them and go to every newsstand, pornography shop and tattoo parlor she could find. The first thing she would do would be to open the centerfolds in those girlie magazines and put tracts in them.

Soon after, some sailor would open one of those magazines. He probably had sounded big and tough the night before, but he knew he was just a 19-year-old boy who was a long way from home. No money. No one to call. Nothing to do but look at that magazine. Then he would find that tract right next to the main attraction and call the person whose name was printed on the tract. That is when things would start happening!

This is just the way it happened, time and time again. That woman rescued those young sailors out of sin. She took them home, prayed for them, fed them, took them to church, cleaned them up and sent them back to the Navy as different young men—by the hundreds.

Was she honored for her work? God honored her. But her church kicked her out because someone saw her coming out of one of those ugly places where she had left her tracts one night.

"Don't you know you're liable to get demon-possessed if you go in there?" she was asked.

"No, I'm not going to get demon-possessed," she answered. "Some little puny demon is not going to run me off—and it ought not run you off either."

Still, she was kicked out of the church, so she started her own church. I preached in it. She didn't want to start her own church, but she had to have a place of worship—and she needed a place to bring the sailors.

She was a mother to many servicemen. Some of them would call her and say, "I don't have any business looking at those dirty, old magazines. I know better than that. I wish you would pray for me. I haven't been acting like I should since I joined the service."

The woman honored God by doing what she was expected to do, instead of acting like a silly, sissy, wimpy, no-faith, dishonorable "Christian." Those sailors were not coming in to the church, so she went out to take the gospel to them and bring them to the Lord. She was kicked out by those who were too upright and uptight to recognize real honor when they saw it.

Through it all, she kept an honorable attitude. And as you live an honorable life before the Lord and the world around you, you'll find your relationships skyrocketing to new levels!

Morning Reflection

What is honor?

_____
_____
_____
_____
_____
_____
_____

Why is it important to live a life of honor among unbelievers?

_____
_____
_____
_____
_____
_____
_____

How did Jesus demonstrate honor?

_____
_____
_____
_____
_____
_____
_____

Today's Connection Points

- **Building Relationships That Last CD: "Holy Are You God" (Track 4)**

As you worship God when listening to this track today, think on how His ways produce freedom in your life.

- **DVD: "Live Holy" (Chapter 4)**

As we draw closer to God, and live for Him completely and honorably, the relationships in our lives become richer and deeper, complete in Him.

- **Love Confessions CD (Track 4)**

Psalms 103:1-5, 143:8; Proverbs 3:12, 15:9; Isaiah 63:8-9; Jeremiah 9:23-24, 31:3; Zephaniah 3:17

Make a quality decision to live a life of honor today.
Keep an honorable attitude in all you do and let it be a witness to all unbelievers around you.

Notes:

_____

_____

_____

_____

_____

_____

_____

_____

_____

_____

_____

_____

_____

_____

_____

_____

_____

_____

_____

_____

_____

_____

_____

_____

_____

_____

_____

_____

_____

_____

_____

_____

_____

_____

_____

_____

_____

_____

_____

Be a Vessel of Honor

by Gloria Copeland

As we talk about living honorably, let's dive into what it means to *be* a vessel of honor. For as we draw closer to Him and live for Him completely and honorably, the relationships in our lives become richer and deeper, complete in Him.

What does it mean to be a vessel of honor? In short, God has called us, as His sons and daughters, to live set apart and sanctified—holy. To be holy simply means that we obey God in everything He tells us to do, that we live for Him and stop participating in the world's ways.

I believe every believer who loves God wants to be holy. But not every believer is actually living holy. Many times we have old habits we've never overcome. We've just lived with them for years.

If you've struggled like this, I know you can be free. God wants you free, and the Scripture says the truth will make you free. If you continue in the Word of God, it will make you free so you can live holy.

Jesus said in His prayer to the Father, "Sanctify them through thy truth: thy word is truth" (John 17:17). I don't care if what's holding you back is the strongest addiction there is, God will set you free. All He needs is your choice, your quality decision that, "No matter what, this is it. I'm leaving bondage behind."

God wants you to do what He says and walk in His ways because those things produce freedom. They produce the best for you. You can't walk in the ways of the world and be free. God loves you. He wants you to be able to wake up every morning happy and full of joy, with your needs met, your family around you and no trouble on any side. And He wants you to be free of all those things you've struggled with for years.

He's Never Stopped Working

You may have given up overcoming some things in your life, but God never has. You may have thought it was impossible, that you'd just have to live with it, whatever it may be. But God has never thought that way. His word to you is always: *All things are possible!*

From the time you came into the kingdom of God, God has endeavored to restore you, to readjust you so that you can walk in the full blessings and the full power of God. He has desired for you to walk holy and unhindered.

Jeremiah 18:1-4 says,

> The word which came to Jeremiah from the Lord: Arise and go down to the potter's house, and there I will cause you to hear My words. Then I went down to the potter's house, and behold, he was working at the wheel. And the vessel that he was making from clay was spoiled in the hand of the potter; so he made it over, reworking it into another vessel as it seemed good to the potter to make it *(The Amplified Bible).*

Ken and I have done a lot of reminiscing about our years in ministry. Looking back, it all seems to have gone by so fast. We've recounted many things that have transpired over the years. And we've remembered mistakes we've made.

But God just kept working and readjusting and restoring and giving us more revelation, so that we could live and think a little higher as we kept going. More than 40 years have come and gone, and He's never left the potter's wheel. He's still working, still forming, still teaching, still training us to live for Him, free from everything that could hold us back from more of Him.

God's doing the same thing for you. You may be at your lowest point ever. You may be thinking you're never going to do anything of worth in this life, never have any relationships that really count. But God has a plan for you. "'For I know the plans I have for you,' declares the Lord, 'plans to prosper you and not to harm you, plans to give you hope and a future'" (Jeremiah 29:11, *New International Version*).

No matter what happens in your life, or where you go, God is on top of the situation.

Because He loves you, He is committed to helping you change.

You Are an Earthen Vessel

We cannot walk in the full blessing of God in our lives or relationships without living a sanctified life. God has a work to do in these last days, and He's going to have a people who are dedicated to Him. He's going to have vessels full of His glory—the glory that He wants to manifest in these last days.

> Hath not the potter power over the clay, of the same lump to make one vessel unto honour, and another unto dishonour? What if God, willing to show his wrath, and to make his power known, endured with much longsuffering the vessels of wrath fitted to destruction: and that he might make known the riches of his glory on the vessels of mercy, which he had afore prepared unto glory (Romans 9:21-23).

According to these verses, there are two kinds of human vessels in the earth. There are vessels of wrath—fitted for destruction, and vessels of mercy—fitted for glory.

The vessels fitted for destruction are people who think they've been getting away with things they've done, but they really haven't gotten away with anything. God has simply endured their sin with longsuffering, giving them opportunity to come to Him.

The vessels of mercy are believers who have been prepared to receive God's end-time manifestations of the glory. We are being set apart. We are the temples of the Holy Ghost. We are the ones who are to keep our bodies separated unto God and away from profane and unholy things. We're to be vessels fitted for glory.

You *Can* Be a Vessel of Honor

As we desire to be vessels fitted for glory, and to live holy, we have to make choices. God will help us, but we have our part to do. Second Timothy 2:15-21 instructs us to:

> Study to show thyself approved unto God, a workman that needeth not to be ashamed, rightly dividing the word of truth. But shun profane and vain babblings: for they will increase unto more ungodliness. And their word will eat as doth a canker.... But in a great house there are not only vessels of gold

and of silver, but also of wood and of earth; and some to honour, and some to dishonour. If a man therefore purge himself from these, he shall be a vessel unto honour, sanctified, and meet for the master's use, and prepared unto every good work.

How is it determined whether we're going to be vessels of honor or vessels of dishonor?

The answer lies in the phrase, "If a man therefore purge himself...."

You do it, and *I* do it. We decide what kind of vessels we'll be. God leaves the choice up to us. He's asking us to purge ourselves from the things that are not right in His sight. He wants us to be free and holy, so we can be vessels of honor.

He is not a God of wrath, but a God of justice. He's like the potter, ever working, ever adjusting, to lead us on a path of righteousness, a path filled with good and with benefits.

Find out what the Word of God says about holiness. Find out what it says about being vessels of honor and dishonor. Begin to do what the Word says. When you do, it will be harder for the evil of the world to stick to you.

Don't focus on what you've struggled with for years anymore. Don't focus on your bad relationships. Don't focus on what you can't do. Focus on what you *can* do—you can spend time in the Word. And as you do, the Word will separate you from the things of this world, the addictions you've been fighting, and the sin with which you've struggled. It will show you which relationships are beneficial for you and which ones are dangerous to your faith.

If you stay with the Word, sooner or later those things will fall away. Those habits will disappear. The desire to stay in ungodly relationships will vanish. You just keep following righteousness. You keep going after God's Word and walking in faith. You keep walking in love and following peace. Fellowship with people who call upon the Lord out of a pure heart, and the first thing you know, those old trappings will be nowhere in sight.

Make your choice today: "I'm going for God. I'm getting rid of this junk hanging on me. I am going after freedom. I'm choosing to be a vessel fitted for glory."

I believe you're willing. I believe you want to be holy. I believe you want to be a temple devoted to the Lord. And as you become His vessel of honor, you'll find your godly relationships will rise to a new level in the Lord.

Evening Reflection

What does it mean to be a vessel of honor?

_____
_____
_____
_____

How is God like a potter at a potter's wheel?

_____
_____
_____
_____

Who determines whether you are a vessel of honor or not?

_____
_____
_____
_____

Notes:

_____
_____
_____
_____
_____
_____
_____
_____
_____
_____
_____
_____
_____
_____
_____
_____
_____
_____
_____
_____
_____
_____
_____
_____
_____

Today's
Prayer of Faith

Father, I purge myself of everything displeasing to You. I want to be a vessel fitted, ready, filled and useful for the glory of God. I make myself available to You, fit and ready for any good work. I offer myself fully to You—spirit, soul and body. Make me a vessel of honor. In Jesus' Name. Amen.

✋ Real-Life Testimonies
to Help Build Your Faith

Set Free by the Truth

When I was in jail I wrote to you and you sent me *From Faith to Faith* and *Pursuit of His Presence.* These are the best gifts I have ever gotten in my life. I just want to thank you and your ministry and Jesus Christ my Savior. John 8:32 says, "You will know the truth and the truth will make you free"—well it did.

My wife had divorced me. She was very hurt for all I had done to her and the kids. I was an alcoholic, cocaine drug addict and unfaithful. She could not believe me when I told her that God had set me free. I prayed and fasted during my prison time. Now we are remarried and serving the Lord together. The Lord worked a miracle in our marriage.

J.G.
Texas

Chapter Five
Living and Giving Honor

Honoring Your Parents
by Gloria Copeland

As another aspect of honor, let's look at a distinct commandment about honor: honoring your parents.

Honoring your parents is very important to God. We're going to look at God's promised blessings to those who honor their parents. But first, let's take a peek at Proverbs 30, where God warns of the danger of *dishonoring* your father and mother.

The First Commandment With a Promise

God can be quite graphic when He wants to get a point across. Look at His description of the person who dishonors his parents: "The eye that mocks a father and scorns to obey a mother, the ravens of the valley will pick it out, and the young vultures will devour it" (Proverbs 30:17, *The Amplified Bible*).

In other words, God is letting us know that it definitely won't go well with us if we don't honor our parents!

On the other hand, God promises great blessings to those who honor their parents: "Children, obey your parents in the Lord [as His representatives], for this is just and right. Honor (esteem and value as precious) your father and your mother—this is the first commandment with a promise—That all may be well with you and that you may live long on the earth (Ephesians 6:1-3, *The Amplified Bible*).

Notice that God's promise ties to the commandment to honor your parents. If you honor, esteem and value them as precious, things will go well with you in this life. Not only that, but God promises you will live long on this earth.

Obey Parents in the Lord

God's command to children is to "Obey your parents *in the Lord.*" That, of course, is speaking of parents who are following God and not parents who are acting contrary to God's Word. Ephesians was written to Christians,

not to the world. For the most part, children in Christian families won't face the kind of difficult situations some children in the world go through.

Many Christian families do face problems, however, between parents and children. In some Christian homes, the father and mother love and honor God, but the children have gone astray and are dishonoring their parents in the process. These children can just count on it: Things will *not* go well with them.

In other Christian families, the parents aren't fulfilling their responsibility to raise their children "[tenderly] in the training and discipline and the counsel and admonition of the Lord" (Ephesians 6:4, *The Amplified Bible*).

The missing ingredient in both these situations is the love of God.

God's Love Makes a Family Work

God's love is the spiritual force that makes a family enjoy life together. Being a member of a family that loves God and one another is the most wonderful blessing. If strife exists in a Christian home between children and their parents, what should a family do? First of all, every parent needs to make the quality decision, *I'm going to walk in love with my children. I won't be overbearing, nor irritate or provoke my children to anger* (Ephesians 6:4, *The Amplified Bible*).

Each child also needs to make a quality decision. They should receive God's Word about honoring their parents and settle it in their hearts: *From now on, I'm going to obey and honor my parents.*

The love of God is the one force that will overcome every strife-filled situation, every age barrier and every generation gap. God's love is what helps a family to work together as a strong unit.

Our family is a strong unit knit together by love. Our children love us; we love them; and they love one another. We're not in strife with one another. We support each other, pray for each other and help each other.

That's the way it should be in every family—the love of God continually manifested in our midst. When acted upon, love will overcome all failures and resistance.

Learning to walk in love has to start somewhere. Parents ought to be forbearing with their children, rearing them tenderly in the admonition of the Lord—always in the love of God. Children ought to be forbearing with their parents, obeying them and showing them honor.

And neither parents *nor* children should wait for the other side to start doing their part first!

Don't be placed in the "class of people who curse their fathers and do not bless their mothers" (Proverbs 30:11, *The Amplified Bible)*. Be counted with those who obey God's command to honor their mother and father. Then you can boldly claim God's promise: "Thank You, Father, that all will go well with me as I live long on this earth!"

Why is the commandment to honor your parents called the first commandment with a promise?

_____
_____
_____
_____
_____
_____
_____
_____

What does it mean to obey your parents "in the Lord"?

_____
_____
_____
_____
_____
_____
_____
_____
_____

How do honor and love work together?

_____
_____
_____
_____
_____
_____
_____
_____

Today's Connection Points

● *Building Relationships That Last* CD: "Unto You" (Track 5)

Give praise to God today for blessing the relationships in your life.

● DVD: "Live & Give Honor" (Chapter 5)

Develop the honor of God in your life. It will begin to work in your heart, your marriage, your business and your career.

● *Love Confessions* CD (Track 5)

Matthew 5:43-44, 46, 22:37-39; Mark 12:33; John 3:35, 5:20, 10:17, 13:1, 34-35, 14:21-24, 15:7-13

Faith in Action

Think about ways you can give honor to your parents, your fellow believers, those in authority over you and those with whom you do business.

Notes:

_____
_____
_____
_____
_____
_____
_____
_____
_____
_____
_____
_____
_____
_____
_____
_____
_____
_____
_____
_____
_____

Being Honorable in Business

by Kenneth Copeland

God wants us—you and me—to do business in honor, in the spirit of the covenant He has given us. In the spirit, we are covenanted together because we are part of the covenant that Jesus has with the Father. This is a lasting relationship we have because we are in Him—in Jesus.

Is Jesus in you? Are you in Him? He is in me, and I am in Him. If you and I are in Him, then we are in Him together. If He is in me and in you, then you are in me and I am in you.

This has some consequences.

For as the body is one, and hath many members, and all the members of that one body, being many, are one body: so also is Christ. For by one Spirit are we all baptized into one body, whether we be Jews or Gentiles, whether we be bond or free; and have been all made to drink into one Spirit. For the body is not one member, but many.... And whether one member suffer, all the members suffer with it; or one member be honoured, all the members rejoice with it. Now ye are the body of Christ, and members in particular (1 Corinthians 12:12-14, 26-27).

The Bible says that all of us together make up the Body of Christ; and if one member of the Body suffers, we all suffer. For me to dishonor you affects not only you, but also me. It affects the whole Body of Christ. If one of us is honored, or honorable, we all share in that honor. Likewise, if one of us dishonors himself, there are negative consequences for all of us.

One Body, One Honor

In Romans 12:10, Paul gives us clear instructions: "Be kindly affectioned one to another with brotherly love; in honour preferring one another."

God has given you the same thing He has given me. I have to respect the fact that you have eternal life, which only God can give. He bestowed it upon you just as He bestowed it upon me. I have to respect you, because I respect God. The Bible says that if we love the Father who begat, we love him also who is begotten of Him (1 John 5:1).

I don't love you because you are lovable, or because you are not lovable. I love you because you are born of God. God has honored you with His life, His Name and His Spirit. How can I do any less? It really makes no difference how I see your conduct—whether I *think* it is right or wrong. I am to deal with *my* conduct, which is regulated by the covenant I have with Almighty God.

God is the only One who has the right to judge. You and I do not. It does not matter if we think the other person is right or wrong. It's none of our business. Whose business is it? God's.

I asked the Lord one time, "What is the biggest problem in the Body of Christ?" I didn't expect to hear what I heard. He answered me quickly, without hesitation: *Your dogged determination to correct one another.* It's the biggest problem in the Body of Christ. It stops more relationships, more healings, more faith, more power, more of everything. Our dogged determination to correct people over whom we have no authority is dishonorable.

Be Honorable, Not Slothful

Paul continues, "[Be] not slothful in business" (Romans 12:11). God does not want us to be slothful in conducting our business. He has honored us by giving it to us. We have to honor our obligation to Him by running that business or doing that job to the best of our ability to do it in faith.

I'll give you an example. God has given me this ministry. He has given me the calling to minister. I have to honor that call and duty. I made a decision that I am going to live responsibly and honorably. I know Jesus wants me to do that, so I am determined to do it.

I promised God that any time I was called on to preach or minister, I would be ready; I would be prepared. That does not mean I want to all the time. It does not mean I am constantly, consistently prayed up and ready to go just on a second's notice. Most of the time I know in advance when I am going to preach. I promised the Lord that I would never take time for myself and my own wants during the periods I should be preparing to minister to other people.

I am responsible for a prophetic ministry. When I travel from place to place on behalf of the Lord, I don't sightsee. I have been all over the world and have hardly seen anything but airports, hotels and convention centers. I don't go for pleasure or relaxation. I don't go to visit or fellowship. I go to do business. I take seriously Jesus' instructions to His disciples as He sent them out to minister. He said, "When you find a worthy house, stay there" (Matthew 10:11, author's paraphrase). I don't run all over town. I come prepared, ready to settle down and attend to business—my Father's business.

I learned this originally from Oral Roberts; then I found it in the Word of God. Later, I saw it in Kenneth E. Hagin and in other anointed men of God.

I have certain time limits that I just won't violate. I may be in your presence sometime, look at my watch and say, "Excuse me, it's time to go." I do that because I am determined to have God's Anointing on me. It is only with the anointing that I can, in turn, be of help to you at all. It is only through the anointing that I can minister effectively to others.

That is the reason all my children are in the ministry. That is the reason there is romance in our family: between Gloria and me, our children and their mates and our grandchildren. My family and I honor the business—the ministry— that God has given us. We honor one another, uplifting one another at all times. As a result we enjoy the blessing of God upon us.

Be Fervent in Spirit

Paul continues, "...fervent in spirit; serving the Lord; rejoicing in hope; patient in tribulation; continuing instant in prayer; distributing to the necessity of saints; given to hospitality. Bless them which persecute you: bless, and curse not" (Romans 12:11-14).

Never lag in zeal or in earnest endeavor. Be aglow and burning with the Spirit, always eagerly and faithfully serving the Lord.

Don't go around with the corners of your mouth hanging down. Put on Jesus. Be like Jesus. Do as He would do.

Rejoice and exult in hope, says the Apostle Paul. Be steadfast and patient in suffering and tribulation. Be constant in prayer.

In this passage Paul is describing the way we are to act in the Body of Christ. We are to keep our mouths shut about our own trials and tribulations, about our own hurts. We are not to go around rehearsing our problems all the time, repeating them to every preacher, minister and counselor we run across—again and again.

One of the reasons that we ministers of the gospel sometimes have to avoid our fellow Christians at meetings is because we cannot stay under the anointing if we constantly and repeatedly are being burdened with other people's trials and tribulations. Many people who do this don't really want help. They just want to go over their problems again and again and again, drawing attention to themselves. That's dishonorable.

God has said that our hurts are very important to Him (1 Peter 5:7). However, they ought to mean little or nothing to us. We should be paying very little attention to our own problems and difficulties other than to take our stand of faith on God's Word and roll our cares over on Him and leave them there. He wants us to be alive with hope, not going around saying that things are hopeless all the time.

Be alive with hope. Be steadfast and patient in suffering. Don't worry about what is coming against you. Be strong in faith. Belittle your problems in the presence of others.

Quit carrying your burdens and cares around everywhere you go. Distribute to the needs of God's people. Share in meeting the necessities of the saints. Pursue the practice of hospitality. Bless those who persecute you, those who are cruel in their attitude toward you. Bless, and do not curse.

As you develop the honor of God in your life, it begins to work in your heart, in your marriage, in your business, in your career. The hard decisions are already made once you decide to live and walk by faith—a life walk. You do your part, God does His part. The devil does his part and runs!

Evening Reflection

How is the Body of Christ connected?

_____
_____
_____
_____

Why is it important for the Body of Christ to honor one another?

_____
_____
_____
_____

How can you be honorable in your business?

_____
_____
_____
_____

Notes

_____
_____
_____
_____
_____
_____
_____
_____
_____
_____
_____
_____
_____
_____
_____
_____
_____
_____
_____
_____
_____
_____

Today's
Prayer of Faith

Father God, I lift my parents, my fellow believers, my government and my business to You. Continue to show me through Your Word how I honor others and live honorably. I am Your vessel of honor. Mold me and shape me. I am Yours!

Real-Life Testimonies
to Help Build Your Faith

Marriage Saved

Being Partners with KCM has been a tremendous blessing to me and my family. I was most impacted in the area of my marriage, as we had been having some problems earlier on, and I definitely wanted out. However, the Lord had been dealing with me to look at myself and not my husband.

When I heard Brother Kenneth's teaching on the love of God and how real love was a choice and not a feeling, I decided to honor God and stay in the marriage. The Lord revealed that when I married my husband I not only made a commitment to him but also to God. My love for the Lord was the motivation to love my husband.

It was not an easy road and my resolve was immediately tested, but I can truly say God has been faithful and our marriage is sweeter now than it has ever been. We recently celebrated our 26th wedding anniversary! To God be the glory. Thanks, Kenneth and Gloria, for being wonderful examples of what marriage and family can be in Christ Jesus.

L.N.
Decatur, Georgia

Chapter Six
Relationship Destroyers

How to Conquer Strife
by Kenneth Copeland

When you're walking in love and forgiveness, living honorably and serving the Lord, you've opened the door for strong, lasting relationships to form in your life. And the enemy won't like that. He will do what he can to stop those relationships from forming by trying to cause strife and discord between you and your brother or sister in Christ.

Let's face it: The fight is on at every level. Strife is separating nation from nation, brother from sister and husband from wife. The conflict comes in varying degrees, from minor disagreements at the office to bomb-dropping border disputes between nations. But one thing is certain: If you live in this world, you're going to have to deal with strife! And, as a believer, you'll have to deal with it in your own life—severely—if you ever want your relationships to last.

Strife isn't something you can treat casually. It's a deadly enemy. James 3:16 says where strife is there is confusion and *every* evil work. Allowing strife to go unchecked or entering into it opens the door to every evil work. A study of the New Testament reveals strife is a deadly enemy that must be stopped in our daily lives.

In fact, as a born-again child of God, you are not only expected to avoid strife, you are expected to be a "peacemaker" (Matthew 5:9). But is it really possible to live in a world that's so full of strife without being drawn into the conflict yourself?

That's a question I used to ask myself a lot. My life used to be full of turmoil and conflict. Even as a boy, I fought over everything—my bike, my clothes—anything. It seemed that I was always fighting!

When I was in grade school I stood out like a sore thumb because all the other boys wore bluejeans and I wore corduroy knickerbockers. So other boys made fun of me by imitating the sound my corduroy britches made as I walked: *Whoosh, whoosh, whoosh, whoosh.* And all the other kids laughed at me. That always started a fight!

It never took much provocation for me to end up in some kind of strife with someone. Even as an adult, I'd look for opportunities to fight. I'd try saying something ugly in an elevator and then watch all the women's ears roll up! Then I'd hope some fellow would say something about it so that maybe I'd get to hit him! I was pretty ornery before I made Jesus the Lord of my life.

Even after I was born again, I could be pretty ornery. But then I fought with my tongue instead of my fist. I said cutting things that packed a more powerful punch than my fist ever had. Instead of slugging a man in the face, I hit him in the heart, which was much more devastating. A black eye will heal in just a few days, but a wounded spirit will fester and fester until someone reaches in with the love of God to heal it.

What I couldn't understand was why I spoke more harshly to my family than to anyone else. It seemed no matter how hard I tried, I couldn't speak a kind word to them. I criticized Gloria's driving so much that she nearly refused to drive while I was with her. And I criticized her flying until she finally decided to just sleep and let old "bad mouth" do all the flying. The way I spoke to my children was no better.

I didn't want to be so insensitive, but I couldn't seem to help it. I had a well-developed habit of speaking harshly and didn't know how to change it. One day I realized that I could hardly remember the last time I had said something kind to my children. That was when I decided that I had to change some things. But how?

Changing the Pattern

I asked the Lord, "How do I change a pattern of behavior that's been part of me for so long?" I knew that Ephesians 4:29 said, "Let no corrupt communication proceed out of your mouth, but that which is good to the use of edifying, that it may minister grace unto the hearers." Harsh words and criticism are certainly not edifying and gracious. I was willing to change this pattern, but I needed a replacement for the things I was so used to saying. I needed something more powerful that would overcome the words of strife and criticism.

I found that alternative in Ephesians 5:3-4: "No coarse, stupid, or flippant talk; these things are out of place; you should rather be thanking God" *(New English Bible)*. The alternative to speaking ugly things is thanksgiving.

I realized I couldn't speak harshly and thank God at the same time. I couldn't criticize those around me if I had a thankful attitude about them.

I immediately decided to put this principle to work in my life. While rushing into my son's room one day, ready to lambaste him about something he had done, I recognized my old behavior pattern. I just stopped and said to myself, *The Word says this kind of behavior is out of place, so I am going to stop and thank God.* I wasn't nearly as angry after I spent a few minutes praising and thanking the Lord for him.

We're not supposed to correct our children in anger. Ephesians 6:4 says: "Fathers, do not irritate and provoke your children to anger [do not exasperate them to resentment], but rear them [tenderly] in the training and discipline and the counsel and admonition of the Lord" *(The Amplified Bible)*. And Ephesians 5:1 says we are to "be…followers of God, as dear children." In other words, we are to imitate God as children imitate their parents.

When *we* miss the mark, God doesn't hit us with a barrage of verbal abuse! Rather, He corrects us with gentle reproof, and that's the way we're to correct our children. When we're angry, if we'll just stop for a few minutes and thank the Lord, it will change the way we discipline them.

This approach will work in *any* situation where there is a temptation to tear into someone with cruel and unkind words. When someone crosses you on the job, at a family gathering, or wherever, instead of letting your mouth be filled with verbal abuse, fill it with praise to God. He is worthy of your praise! If you are thinking about how good God is, you can't be talking about how bad others are!

Imitating God

How did Jesus respond to unlovely people? He imitated His heavenly Father and spoke the Word of God. He said, "The words I speak are not My own. I only say what the Father tells Me to say" (see John 8:28). And John 3:34 tells us that because He only spoke the Word of God,

He had the Spirit in an unlimited measure. The power of God was Jesus' vindication in every situation—not smart-aleck words! He didn't use *any* flippant words. He only said what the Father told Him to say.

In Ephesians 4:29-32, we find the kinds of things the Father is telling *us* to say:

> Let no corrupt communication proceed out of your mouth, but that which is good to the use of edifying, that it may minister grace unto the hearers. And grieve not the holy Spirit of God, whereby ye are sealed unto the day of redemption. Let all bitterness, and wrath, and anger, and clamour, and evil speaking, but put away from you, with all malice: And be ye kind one to another, tenderhearted, forgiving one another, *even as* God for Christ's sake hath forgiven you.

Notice the words *even as.* We are supposed to imitate God no matter what the circumstances. We are supposed to be acting like God, speaking His words and doing His work.

If we keep ourselves busy doing His thing, we won't have time to do *our* thing! We will be so full of God's love, there won't be any room for strife. That's the key to having the power of God manifest in our lives just as it was manifest in Jesus' life.

The way I renew my mind to the love of God is to study and meditate 1 Corinthians 13:4-8, *New King James Version.* I read it in the first person like this: "I suffer long and am kind. I do not envy; I do not parade myself. I am not puffed up. I do not behave rudely; I do not seek my own way; I am not provoked. I think no evil; I do not rejoice in iniquity, but I rejoice in the truth. I bear all things, I believe all things, I hope all things and I endure all things. I never fail." This is a valid confession because God is love, and I am born of God. Therefore, I am born of love.

When an unlovely person tries to provoke you into strife, you will remember, *I am not provoked.* Instead of retaliating, let love come out of your mouth. You have not only taken a defensive action against strife, but an offensive action as well!

Beginning today, you can conquer strife. Make a decision to keep yourself full of the love of God. Meditate on the "love chapter" (1 Corinthians 13:4-8). Confess it in the first person several times a day. And when others provoke you, don't retaliate. Instead, give thanks to God for His goodness and watch His presence come on the scene. Put strife under your feet where it belongs!

Morning Reflection

Why is strife so dangerous?

_____
_____
_____
_____
_____
_____
_____

How can you stop strife in its tracks?

_____
_____
_____
_____
_____
_____
_____

What does it mean to imitate God?

_____
_____
_____
_____
_____
_____

Today's Connection Points

- **_Building Relationships That Last_ CD: "It's All About Love" (Track 6)**

  As you listen to this track, focus on allowing the love of God to operate through you today.

- **DVD: "Keep the Commandment of Love" (Chapter 6)**

  When you walk in love you open the door for strong, lasting relationships to form in your life.

- **_Love Confessions_ CD (Track 6)**

  John 16:23-27, 17:20-26; Romans 5:5, 8, 8:28, 35-39, 12:9-10, 13:8-10

Faith in Action

Stop strife before it starts!

Walk in love and an attitude of thankfulness, and watch God move.

Notes:

_____

_____

_____

_____

_____

_____

_____

_____

_____

_____

_____

_____

_____

_____

_____

_____

_____

_____

_____

_____

_____

_____

_____

_____

_____

_____

_____

_____

_____

_____

_____

_____

_____

_____

_____

_____

_____

Envy: The Devil's Personal Poison
by Gloria Copeland

Envy: "A feeling of discontent and ill will because of another's advantages, possessions or success."

It's an experience we've all had at one time or another. It is so common, in fact, most people think it is no big deal. They see it as just a harmless, human emotion. But they are gravely mistaken—and it can ruin relationships.

As innocent as it may sometimes seem, envy is actually the devil's own poison, designed to turn love into hate and immobilize the force of faith in your life. Once you understand how dangerous it is, you'll want to rid yourself of it once and for all.

"Well, Gloria, that shouldn't be too difficult for me," you may say. "I don't really think I'm envious of anyone."

That may be true. But let me encourage you to search your heart carefully just to be sure, because many times we aren't even conscious of envy. We may feel it stirring within us, but we fail to identify it because we assume such feelings are "only natural."

Actually, "natural" is precisely what envy is. It's part of what the Bible calls the "natural" or "carnal" mind. It's a mind programmed by the devil to be in direct opposition to God.

Another biblical term for it is "the flesh." Envy is listed with "works of the flesh" in Galatians 5, and is put alongside some other, very serious sins such as: "Adultery, fornication, uncleanness, lasciviousness, Idolatry, witchcraft, hatred, variance, emulations, wrath, strife, seditions, heresies, envyings, murders, drunkenness, revellings, and such like" (verses 19-21).

That's not exactly a pretty list, is it?

Most believers would never purposely engage in any of those fleshly activities. How then does envy get into our lives?

It slips in unnoticed.

Suppose you go to church, for instance, and you see Brother Smith with a new car. Suddenly a thought comes to your mind: *Why does he have a new car? He didn't even need it. I'm the one who needs a new car.*

Or suppose you see Sister Jones in a beautiful, new dress. As you sit down next to her, you notice how dowdy your dress is compared to hers. Suddenly you feel like someone's ugly stepsister.

You may not think much more about it—consciously. But later, you notice you're a little irritated or depressed. You can't quite put your finger on why you feel that way. After all, you were having a good day. What happened?

Envy crept in and poisoned you with a feeling of ill will and discontent because of another's success or advantages. Envy made a move on you.

Pulling the Plug on Your Faith

Notice I said it made a move *on* you, not *in* you. That's an important distinction.

You see, if you're a born-again believer, envy is not a part of your spiritual nature. It's something the devil tries to pressure you into receiving. He dangles it in front of you like bait on a hook, hoping you'll take a bite.

Why? Because he wants to defeat you! He wants to keep you sick, broke, sad and perpetually trapped beneath your circumstances. And to do that, he must somehow stop you from living by faith.

Since he can't very well just come barreling in the front door and steal the faith right out of your heart, he slips in the back way. He uses envy and strife to interrupt the flow of love in your life. The minute love is disrupted, your faith stops working too, because faith works by love (Galatians 5:6).

Many Christians don't understand that principle, so they struggle along, quarreling and fussing with one another—and all the while wonder why their faith isn't producing results and their relationships are falling apart. They don't realize that if you want to walk in the power and blessing of God, you cannot allow envy or strife into your life. Period.

James 3:16 shows us why that's true. It says, "Where envying and strife is, there is confusion and every evil work." In other words, envy and strife give the devil an open door into your life.

Even When You're Right... You're Wrong

No wonder the Apostle John warns us so strongly against it, saying:

> This is the message...which you have heard from the first, that we should love one another, [And] not be like Cain who [took his nature and got his motivation] from the evil one and slew his brother.... He who does not love abides (remains, is held and kept continually) in [spiritual] death. Anyone who hates...his brother [in Christ] is [at heart] a murderer, and you know that no murderer has eternal life abiding (persevering) within him (1 John 3:11-12, 14-15, *The Amplified Bible*).

Envy started with Cain and Abel, and it's clearly serious business—in that case it led to murder. We need to rid ourselves of it completely and start loving each other. We need to stop striving with each other and "lay [our] lives down for [those who are our] brothers [in Him]" (verse 16, *The Amplified Bible*).

That's what real love is, you know—laying down your life for someone else. And in a very real sense, you are laying down your life when you refuse to envy, because envy tries to get you to fight for your own rights. It pushes you to look out for your own welfare and to be hostile because someone else is more successful in life than you are.

Ironically, however, what envy actually does is stop your success. It keeps you from rising to the level of those you are envying. Why? Because, as I said before, it stops your faith. It takes you outside the realm of love— and therefore becomes a trap that secures your failure!

The truth is, all strife works that way— whether it's caused by envy or by something else. All strife is sin!

That means even when you are on the "right" side of an argument, if you're in strife, you're wrong. When you're offended and angry with your husband or wife, your

children or anyone else, you're wrong. You've opened the door to the devil and you'd better do something quickly.

What should you do?

Shut the door! Stubbornly resist those fleshly pressures and temptations of the devil. Treat strife just as you'd treat a rattlesnake or any other deadly invader. Refuse to let it in!

If you're a preacher of the gospel, for instance, and there's a new pastor in town who is getting more results than you are, don't be naive enough to fall into the trap that envy is setting. Trick the devil! Turn the tables on him! Start praising God for the success of the new pastor. Do what you can to help him.

In other words, start walking in love and laying down selfishness. If you'll do that, you'll keep the door open for the blessings of God on your relationships and in every area of life.

You Can Do It!

That's important because in this dangerous day, we need God's blessings more than ever. It's time we quit allowing the devil to darken our homes, our businesses, our churches and our individual lives with strife and envy. It's time we quit letting him pull the plug on our faith power. It's time we started living in the light.

You may be thinking, *That's easier said than done!*

I know. But you can do it.

How? Learn to watch over yourself. Pay attention to your state of mind. When you find yourself depressed or downcast, don't just ignore those feelings. Think back. Ask yourself, "What started this downturn?"

You may realize that a particular situation sparked feelings of aggravation, jealousy or strife within you. If so, look at that situation through the eyes of God and then talk to it (see Mark 11:23).

Say, "That situation has no power over me. I refuse to allow it to bring envy and strife into my life. I yield to the forces of love and joy within me. And, Lord, I praise You for Brother Smith's new car. I thank You that Sister Jones has those nice clothes!"

Then just start praising the Lord. Before long, the love of God will be bubbling up out of your heart again and you'll be singing in genuine joy!

Evening
Reflection

What is envy?

_____
_____
_____
_____

How can envy pull the plug on your faith and hinder your relationships?

_____
_____
_____
_____

How can you shut the door to envy?

_____
_____
_____
_____

Notes:

_____
_____
_____
_____
_____
_____
_____
_____
_____
_____
_____
_____
_____
_____
_____
_____
_____
_____
_____
_____
_____
_____

Today's
Prayer of Faith

Father, today I stand in the Name of Jesus, choosing to love, choosing to put envy and strife behind me. I don't want to give the enemy any place in my relationships. Holy Spirit, when envy or strife arises, help me to identify it quickly and turn the situation around by living a life of thanksgiving and praise. Thank You for being my Guide, so that I may live a blessed life! Amen.

Real-Life Testimonies
to Help Build Your Faith

Set Free at Southwest

I just want to praise the Lord for the Southwest Believers' Convention this past year.

I'm a truck driver and was saved when I was 10 years old. However I had been involved in pornography and adulterous relationships over the past 15 years. In my profession I have every opportunity to look at magazines, movies, and sleep with women other than my wife. I hated who I had become. I even blamed God for allowing it to happen and didn't think He would forgive me. Thankfully, my wife stuck by me through it all.

On July 12, 2002, I distinctly heard the Lord say, *Go to the Believers' Convention in Fort Worth.* I came home and told my wife and she was all for it. Everything just fell into place—airline, hotel and car rental prices—I couldn't believe it! God made the way for me to come to Fort Worth. During the service, it was as if all the speakers were talking to *me!!* I knew then that my God in heaven did love me and still wanted me back!

I was set free August 8, 2002, and since returning home I have been renewing my mind by the washing of the Word. I thank you for listening to God because I was lost in life but now I AM FOUND!

R.B.
Randleman, North Carolina

Chapter Seven
Raising Children

Raising Children in Perverse Times

by Gloria Copeland

Your children are precious to you. The Scripture calls them a heritage and a reward. You love them so much that you want them to grow and mature into happy, healthy, successful adults. But do you love them enough to train them the way God says in His Word, to be an example to them and even to correct them?

If you are a parent, God has commanded you to teach and train your children in His Word and His ways so that they can live a victorious life. It's not an option. It's a responsibility that each of us as parents will have to answer for.

Genesis 18:19 indicates that God chose Abraham because He knew Abraham would teach his children to keep the ways of the Lord. It's evident this is very important to God.

We live in a time when the world is getting darker and it is becoming more of a challenge to live holy. Even those who are saved can find themselves bombarded with all kinds of ungodly, perverse sights and sounds from television, movies, magazines, the Internet—you name it. If adults are being challenged with negative input and temptation, just think what kind of environment today's children are growing up in. If they don't have strong parental direction and training, the enemy is sure to have free reign in their lives. Taking your place as a godly parent has never been more important.

The enemy wants to control the lives of as many people as he can. He does this by tricking them into going his way. He is peddling murder, hate and every kind of ungodly, immoral thing you can think of. If he can get those kinds of things before a person's eyes and in their ears, he will have a place in their life.

Unfortunately, even some Christians are opening the door to the enemy by taking part in the world's unclean entertainment and activities. They may think it won't hurt them, but people can't feed on the world's trash and not be affected.

If we don't fight the good fight of faith (1 Timothy 6:12), the devil will come in and take over our homes and our children. And remember, when he comes in, he brings the curse with him. We must fight to keep our homes devil-free!

Be Ye Separate

Do you realize that consistently living a holy lifestyle has everything to do with how your children turn out? If you go to church and talk right and look good in front of people, but then you live differently at home, you are making it very hard for your children to take God seriously. As they are growing up, children learn more by watching what you do than by listening to what you say. And they never forget what they observe at home.

Holiness is letting God separate you out of the darkness of the world into a life that is worth living—a life lived in Him.

> Be ye not unequally yoked together with unbelievers: for what fellowship hath righteousness with unrighteousness? and what communion hath light with darkness?…or what part hath he that believeth with an infidel? And what agreement hath the temple of God with idols? for ye are the temple of the living God; as God hath said, I will dwell in them, and walk in them…. Wherefore come out from among them, and be ye separate, saith the Lord, and touch not the unclean thing… (2 Corinthians 6:14-17).

The word *separate* means "to set apart, to disunite, to divide, to part company, to go in a different direction, to cease to be associated with, to become distinct or disengaged, as cream separates from milk."

So to get a picture of how we're to live, think about how cream rises to the top and is separated from the plain milk.

That's exactly what we have to do in regard to the sin the world is endeavoring to sell us on every hand. We must rise above it by doing what

Romans 12:2 says: "Be not conformed to this world: but be ye transformed by the renewing of your mind...."

We're not just choosing for our own lives when we make choices. Deuteronomy 30:19 says, "I have set before you life and death, blessing and cursing: therefore choose life, that both thou and thy seed may live." The decisions we make not only affect us—they also affect our children.

Raising the Next Generation

If God wants you to be separated, how much more important is it for your children to be separated from the vile things of the world? Little children are being taught from elementary school that homosexuality is OK—it's an "alternative lifestyle." They are being taught that they can choose to do whatever makes them happy. Generations of children are growing up without God in their lives, without boundaries. They have no Ten Commandments to live by, no basis for morality.

But it doesn't have to be that way in your family—and it shouldn't be. Over and over the Bible commands parents to teach their children the Word of God (Deuteronomy 6:6-7, 11:18-21). That will make all the difference in what kind of people they grow up to be.

If you fail to teach your children what God's Word says is moral or immoral, you can be sure the world will teach them what it believes. If your children attend public school, you may have to deal with a lot of issues earlier than you would choose. Watch carefully what others are depositing into your children. Talk to their teachers. Ask them what materials they use. Talk to your children and monitor what they are hearing and seeing.

In Leviticus 18, God deals with homosexuality and other sexual sins. He also makes it plain that His people are not to mingle among the heathen and learn their ways.

First Corinthians 15:33 adds, "Do not be so deceived and misled! Evil companionships (communion, associations) corrupt and deprave good manners and morals and character" *(The Amplified Bible)*.

And James 4:4 goes on to say, "... whosoever therefore will be a friend of the world is the enemy of God."

These are important lessons to teach your children, considering the kind of peer pressure they are sure to experience in today's world.

It's also important to train your children to walk with God on a daily basis by reading the Word, praying and spending time with Him. Teach them to desire spiritual things and help them learn to "walk in the Spirit, and [they] shall not fulfil the lust of the flesh" (Galatians 5:16).

Certainly, I haven't covered everything you should teach your children from the Word. There's so much more. But remember this: Your victory is tied up in your obedience. Obeying God's Word and teaching your children to do the same will ensure the future of your family.

When you choose a church, think about your children as well as yourself. There are many good churches with excellent children's training. Get your children involved in these programs.

Most of all, be mindful that living a godly life before your children is the best teacher! So provide a solid home with love and support, and show them by example how to live separated unto God. Let them see how you respond when bad news or trouble comes. Let them see your faith in action. Let them see how you handle all kinds of circumstances—they will never escape that influence.

They might forget your words, but they won't forget your ways. And if you want to have long, lasting, godly relationships with your children, it's time to step up to the plate. The reward far outweighs the cost!

Morning Reflection

What does it mean to "be separate" from the world?

_____
_____
_____
_____
_____

What effect does your lifestyle have on your children?

_____
_____
_____
_____
_____

What is your responsibility when it comes to teaching your children?

_____
_____
_____
_____
_____
_____
_____

Today's Connection Points

- **_Building Relationships That Last_ CD: "God Is My Light" (Track 7)**

   As you worship God today, thank Him that He is your protection and you have nothing to fear.

- **DVD: "Raising Children Without Fear" (Chapter 7)**

   When you become rooted and grounded in love, there is no room for fear. Every prayer and thought for your children will be love-based and faith-based.

- **_Love Confessions_ CD (Track 7)**

   1 Corinthians 2:9, 8:3; 2 Corinthians 5:14-15, 9:7, 13:11, 14; Galatians 2:20, 5:6, 13-14; Galatians 5:22-23

Love your children through your actions and example.
Choose to get involved, and raise them in faith, not fear!

Notes:

_____
_____
_____
_____
_____
_____
_____
_____
_____
_____
_____
_____
_____
_____
_____
_____
_____
_____
_____
_____
_____
_____
_____
_____
_____
_____
_____
_____
_____
_____
_____
_____
_____
_____
_____
_____
_____
_____
_____
_____
_____

Raising Children Without Fear
by Kenneth Copeland

A number of years ago, singer and songwriter Johnny Cash recorded the song, "A Boy Named Sue." While this song is meant to be lighthearted and humorous, it also speaks volumes about how parents can fall into the trap of trying to control and manipulate their children.

In this particular song, a rough-and-tough father who is about to abandon his family decides to name his son *Sue* in an effort to toughen him up and cause him to become a "real man."

As expected, the boy ends up fighting his way through life because of the shame of having a girl's name.

While this father's plan did make his son tough, it did not build strong character in him. Beating the daylights out of everyone who crosses you doesn't make you strong.

The strongest men are not men of violence. They are men who know how to love with the love of God.

It Worked for Mama...*Or Did It?*

In the same way the father in "A Boy Named Sue" used shame and humiliation to toughen up his son, parents today—like countless generations of parents before them—have used *fear* to try and change or control the behavior of their children.

For instance, how many times have you heard or said something like this: "Now, sweetheart, don't run out into the street like that again. Daddy is afraid you will get hit by a car."

That's fear—pure and simple. It is using fear to manipulate your child into doing what you want him or her to do. What's more, by saying those kinds of things, you are raising your child in a spirit of fear.

"Oh, but Brother Copeland, how else is a child going to learn to watch out for cars and be safe? Everyone knows in a situation like this that a little fear might be healthy."

That's a lie from the devil. There is *never* a time when a little fear—or a lot for that matter—is healthy.

Revelation 21:8 exposes the deception in that kind of thinking: "But the fearful, and unbelieving, and the abominable, and murderers, and whoremongers, and sorcerers, and idolaters, and all liars, shall have their part in the lake which burneth with fire and brimstone: which is the second death."

Fear, doubt, abominations, murder, whoremongering, sorcery, idolatry, lying—not one of these is healthy. Not in the slightest. And notice where *fear* is on this list of undesirables—at the very top.

The truth is, you really have no desire for your children to be afraid, or *fear-full*. No parent does. You wouldn't have your children terrorized every time they see a car coming. You simply would like for them to develop enough sound judgment about cars to stay out of the street and not get hit.

But parents often fall back on fear to try and get the job done. Why? Because that's the way their parents raised them, which was how their parents raised them and how their parents raised them. Out of ignorance, generation after generation has sown fear into its children. And generation after generation has reaped that fear.

Granted, children do need information to help them succeed in life. But they also need to be taught how to walk by faith—and not just in potentially dangerous situations, such as getting hit by a car. They need to be shown how to take the Word of God and use it to meet any situation head-on and overcome it—not run from it.

When Parents Get Out of Control

To break a cycle of fear in your life and in the lives of your children, you need to go first to the Lord and ask Him if you are indeed promoting and imparting a spirit of fear to your children. If you are, repent of it before God. It's not your job to control and change people anyway—not even your own children. And you certainly should not be trying to do it through fear.

We are reminded in 2 Timothy 1:7 that "God hath not given us the spirit of fear; but of power, and of love, and of a sound mind." Since God did not give us a spirit of fear, we have no business promoting it or using it as a tool, especially where our children are concerned.

If your children are going to have sound judgment and sound decision-making skills, then you must take time to teach them. You are going to have to invest quality time in them. One of the reasons there's been so much failure in raising children is because parents are not taking the time to love them through prayer. By that I mean setting aside a designated time to pray for them and hold them before the Lord.

Now I'm not talking about crying out, "Oh God, can't You help me with these kids? I'm afraid they're going to jail. I just know they're doing drugs."

No, that's a prayer based in fear. It's praying out of torment, and the results it will produce are disastrous. That kind of praying will connect you to the terrible things you are afraid of.

The kind of prayer I'm talking about is moments of quietness when you call the names of your children before God and purposely begin to love them from your heart with "the love of God [that] is shed abroad in our hearts by the Holy Ghost…" (Romans 5:5). Through prayer, bathe them in faith and love—after all, faith works by love (Galatians 5:6).

So instead of fretful, tormented prayers, pray something like this: "Lord, I love my son and I'm holding him before You right now. I see You holding him in Your arms, ministering life, peace and comfort to him. Lord, I realize that You love him far more than I ever could. And Father, I pray for the peace of God that passes all understanding to stand guard over his heart and mind. Help him, Lord, to be full of You, to know You, and to worship You. And Father, help me see my son the way You see him. Help me love him with Your love."

As a word of caution, when you begin praying this way, it may seem a little shallow at first. But remember, love at its most shallow point is deeper than anything else.

If you desire to see your children develop strong godly character, love them with the love that He has imparted to your heart as a parent. And realize that His love is not merely human love, it's supernatural Love—Himself.

Allow that love to grow, expand and develop until you become rooted and grounded in love, that you might be filled with all the fullness of God (Ephesians 3:17-19). Once you are filled with the fullness of God, there is no room for fear. Every prayer you pray for your children...every thought of them...will be love-based and faith-based.

And love never fails.

Evening Reflection

In what ways do many parents raise their children in fear?

_____
_____
_____
_____
_____
_____

Think of a situation where you have taught your children with fear. How would you approach that differently now?

_____
_____
_____
_____
_____
_____

What's the difference between a fear-based prayer and a faith-based prayer?

Notes:

Today's
Prayer of Faith

Father God, I lift my children before You today. Thank You that You give Your angels charge over my children to keep and guard them in all their ways, and that Your peace that passes all understanding stands guard over their hearts and minds in Christ Jesus. I believe I receive Your wisdom to raise them in the nurture, training and instruction of the Lord through my words and example. Help me to see them the way You see them and love them with Your love. I commit to love them through prayer and in all I do. Thank You that my children know and worship You, are filled with Your love, and are mighty in faith! In Jesus' Name. Amen.

Real-Life Testimonies
to Help Build Your Faith

The Word Brings the Answer

We had been married for 10 years and our greatest desire was to have children of our own, but it hadn't happened. However, the Lord showed my husband our child so he knew God was going to do it.

In 1997 the Lord told me He was not first in my life. He told me to put Him first and He would answer all my prayers. So I started to seek His face and that made a great difference in my life. The desire to have children was not gone, but it was in the right place.

The day came that friends told us about Kenneth and Gloria Copeland. We started to read the *Believer's Voice of Victory* magazine and watch the broadcast. We learned to speak God's Word instead of the things we felt and saw.

The last time we wrote you, we asked you to pray and stay in agreement with us for having children. But there was one thing we didn't know—I was already pregnant! I am now 20 weeks pregnant and we are doing fine. We believe this child is blessed by the Lord, healthy in spirit, soul and body.

We love and thank you for all your prayers.

J.R.
The Netherlands

Chapter Eight
Standing for Rebellious Children

Dealing With Rebellious Children
by Kenneth Copeland

Like most parents, Gloria and I had to deal with the problem of rebellion in our children. We realized that it had to be stopped quickly before it developed into a serious situation.

Don't be guilty of ignoring symptoms of rebellion when your children are small. Don't simply excuse it as a stage they are going through and think they will grow out of it. If you ignore it when they are small, it will be much more difficult to handle when they get older and the rebellion has had time to develop into a strong force. Stopping rebellion now helps prevent a rift between your future relationship together… and your child's relationship with the Lord.

Facing Challenges

But what do you do when your children are getting deeper into trouble every day? When our children rebelled, especially as teenagers, it wasn't always easy. Today, our children are serving the Lord with all their hearts, but it took awhile to get there.

There were times when we wanted to break down and cry or lose our tempers or do something in the natural, but we would remember Jeremiah 31:16-17: "Thus saith the Lord; Refrain thy voice from weeping, and thine eyes from tears: for thy work shall be rewarded, saith the Lord; and they [your children] shall come again from the land of the enemy. And there is hope in thine end, saith the Lord, that thy children shall come again to their own border."

Mothers, take God's Word for it. Receive Jeremiah 31:16-17 for yourself. Stop weeping for your children and start believing the Word. That's the only thing that will bring them around.

Fathers, I am speaking to you too! It's time for the fathers to get involved in the spiritual activities of their families. For too long, the women have carried more than their share of family responsibility. Husbands and fathers, get on your knees before God and accept your place as head of your household. You are the prophet of God to your family. This is not a lightweight thing; it takes a commitment on your part to fulfill your responsibilities. Get yourself straight before God, then see to your children. If necessary, go to your kids and ask their forgiveness for neglecting them.

I have had to learn these things the hard way, and I know what I am talking about. If you're ready to stand for your kids, here are the steps we followed to find victory for our children:

Step 1: Faith, Not Fear

First of all, you must start being moved by faith. You can't get anything accomplished as long as you allow fear and worry to dominate your thinking. Stop the negative flow by starting to think and talk what the Word of God says about your children instead of dwelling on the problems you see in their lives.

Isaiah 54:13, for instance, says that all your children shall be taught of the Lord, and great shall be their peace. Receive that promise for your children. Start believing it and speaking it. Then, find other promises and use them to build a foundation of faith.

Stand on Psalm 112:1-2: "Praise ye the Lord. Blessed is the man that feareth the Lord, that delighteth greatly in his commandments. His seed shall be mighty upon earth: the generation of the upright shall be blessed."

Deuteronomy 28:4 says, "The fruit of your womb will be blessed" *(New International Version)*.

Gloria and I stood on verses like these many years ago for our children. We saw the devil trying to get a foothold in their lives, so one weekend we got our concordance and four or five translations of the Bible. We began to search out scriptures and write out agreement prayers concerning our children.

We stood on that Word, took authority in the spirit world and refused to give Satan any room to operate. We started saying, "Thank God, our children are not going to hell. Thank

God, they are taught of the Lord and great is their peace!" Instead of walking the floor and worrying about the problem, we walked the floor and praised God for the solution.

Step 2: Bind the Enemy

The second thing you need to do is bind the devil with the Word of God and tell him he can't have your children. *This is our responsibility as Christian parents.* A child does not understand the spiritual forces coming against him, so it is up to the parents to fight the spiritual battles and keep Satan out of the child's life.

Then follow the instructions Jesus gave in Matthew 9:38 to pray the Lord of the harvest would send out laborers into the field who can reach your children.

God knows your children better than they know themselves. He knows who they'll listen to, and He knows how to bring those people into your children's lives at just the right time.

Step 3: Rejoice!

The third thing you need to do is to start rejoicing in the Lord. You'll study more about this in Gloria's session this evening. Zechariah 10:7-8 says, "They of Ephraim shall be like a mighty man, and their heart shall rejoice as through wine: Yea, their children shall see it, and be glad; their heart shall rejoice in the Lord. I will hiss for them, and gather them; for I have redeemed them...."

Can you see the sequence there?

When parents rejoice in the Lord, the children will see it and be glad. *Then* God signals for them and redeems them.

Your job is to rejoice in the Lord yourself, to cast all your cares on Him. You may not even know where your children are right now. But God knows and this scripture says He will signal for them and they'll return. It doesn't matter where they are. You probably weren't exactly in your prayer closet when God first found you either, were you? I know I wasn't. But He found us anyway and pulled us to Himself.

Step 4: Be Open to Change

The fourth thing you need to do—and this may well be the most crucial—is this: When you're praying for your children, be sure to ask God to change you as well.

I know parents who've gone through these steps, praying that God would send their children back and He did. But when they got back home, the parents hadn't changed a bit. They jumped right in the middle of them and ran them off again.

Don't let that happen. Instead, soak your heart in the gentleness and the compassion of God. Let God turn you into someone so full of the love of Jesus and so full of His presence that your kids don't want to leave home.

Step 5: Don't Let Go

Even with all this, be warned, your children may not turn around overnight. So until they do, be like Abraham and call things that be not as though they were. Say, "I'm not moved by what I see or hear. I'm not moved by what I feel. I'm moved by what I believe and I believe what God says!" Say that aloud along with the scriptures you've found—not just occasionally but literally night and day. Then dig in your heels and stand.

Second Peter 2:9 says that God knows how to deliver. He knows how to do it, so give Him the opportunity. It doesn't matter where your children are—in the room or a thousand miles away. You don't have to be in their presence to take authority over Satan.

Grab hold of God's Word and refuse to let go of it where your children are concerned...sooner or later, that Word will grab hold of them!

Morning  Reflection

What is our responsibility as Christian parents in dealing with rebellion?

_____

_____

_____

_____

_____

_____

What steps are necessary to bring back a rebellious child?

_____

_____

_____

_____

_____

_____

What scriptures stood out to you that you can stand on in faith?

_____

_____

_____

_____

_____

_____

_____

Today's Connection Points

⊙ *Building Relationships That Last* CD: "Where I Belong" (Track 8)

As you are worshiping God today, purpose to be get into His place of peace.

⊙ DVD: *Stand For Your Children In Faith* (Chapter 8)

Start thinking and speaking what God's Word says about your children instead of dwelling on the problems you see in their lives.

⊙ *Love Confessions* CD (Track 8)

Ephesians 1:4-9, 2:4-10, 4:1-3, 4:15-16, 5:1-2, 6:23-24; Philippians 1:9-11, 2:1-3; Colossians 2:1-3

Faith  in Action

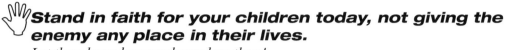 **Stand in faith for your children today, not giving the enemy any place in their lives.**

Let them know how much you love them!

Notes:

_____
_____
_____
_____
_____
_____
_____
_____
_____
_____
_____
_____
_____
_____
_____
_____
_____
_____
_____
_____
_____
_____
_____
_____
_____
_____
_____
_____
_____
_____
_____
_____
_____
_____
_____
_____
_____
_____
_____

When God Says, *"Pssst!"*

by Gloria Copeland

Did you know your children are in your heart? It's true. You carry your children in your heart the same way God carries you in His heart.

You can feel what's going on with them even when they're on the other side of the world. If they're hurt, if they're lonely, if they're toying with sin and getting off track—when things are wrong or things are right, you can feel it.

I remember once when Ken and I were in Australia. We were flying from one city to another and suddenly thoughts of our son, John, flooded my heart. John was a teenager at the time and he was *all boy.* He rode everything with wheels—cars, trucks, motorcycles, dune buggies. And it seemed he was always turning something over.

That day on the plane, I was concerned about him. I knew how much the devil would like to sneak in and steal his life, and I was concerned that John's misadventures could give the devil the opportunity to do it.

But the Holy Spirit broke in on my thoughts. He spoke to Ken and said, *My mercy hovers over John.* When Ken relayed those words to me, all my fears vanished.

My mercy hovers over John. I'll never forget that promise. As I've prayed for John throughout the years, that wonderful word from God has often risen up and reminded me that his life is secure. It would assure me that God would keep him and hold him steady until the day he got things straight in his life.

My mercy hovers over your child. That is a wonderful word from God. If God will do that for my child, He will do it for yours. The covenant God has made with you in the blood of Jesus extends to your children and your children's children. Psalm 103:17 says, "But the mercy of the Lord is from everlasting to everlasting upon them that fear him, and his righteousness unto children's children."

Our grandchildren are covered in our covenant with God. Everything God gives to me, He'll give to them. All the protection I have, He passes on to my family.

If you're a believer and willing to trust God for the deliverance and salvation of your children, you'll not be disappointed.

"Come Here"

In connection with this, let's take a closer look at Zechariah 10:7-9, which Ken shared with you this morning. In those verses, God tells us about the outpouring of the Spirit of God in the last days—the days we're living in. He says:

> And they of Ephraim shall be like a mighty man, and their heart shall rejoice as through wine: yea, their children shall see it, and be glad; their heart shall rejoice in the Lord. I will hiss for them [your children], and gather them; for I have redeemed them.... And I will sow them among the people: and they shall remember me in far countries; and they shall live with their children, and turn again.

You may not even know where your children are right now. They may be in another city or another country. It doesn't matter. This scripture says when you rejoice in the Lord—not when you're depressed or worried or afraid, but when you trust God so totally that you're filled up with joy—then your children will see it and turn.

"I will hiss for them." What does that mean? It means God will signal for them. He'll say, *Pssst! Come here!* And they'll come running.

Let me tell you something. God knows how to get someone's attention. He knows how to signal for the ones His people are praying for. Kenneth's mother prayed for me and then one day God said, *Pssst, Gloria!* I heard Him and was born again.

I didn't know much about God before that time. I knew there was a God, but had no real knowledge about Him. Yet, He still knew how to get my attention. He called, and here I am today preaching His Word!

He'll do the same thing for your child. It doesn't matter what kind of wickedness that child has fallen into, God can still reach him.

I know a man who pastors a great church in Sacramento, California. His name is Phil Goudeaux. He used to be part of the militant black power movement. In fact, he was in charge of security for the Black Panthers.

He didn't know God and he didn't want to know God. But one day when he was in college, a young, white fellow came over to his lunch table and started telling him about Jesus. This Black Panther leader couldn't believe it. The nerve of this guy! He tried to get rid of him. He threatened him and even tried to hit him...but he couldn't.

For weeks this little, white fellow followed this big, "bad" black guy around talking to him about Jesus. Finally, the Black Panther prayed with the fellow just to get him off his back. After that he tried to forget about it...but he couldn't. Two weeks later, all by himself, he made Jesus Christ the Lord of his life. Today he preaches salvation to others.

Apprehending Paul

God knows how to get someone's attention! He'll knock them over and speak to them right out loud if He needs to. He proved that in the life of a man named Saul. Years after that man was saved, he wrote, "...I follow after, if that I may apprehend that for which also I am apprehended of Christ Jesus" (Philippians 3:12).

God apprehended Paul one day on the road to Damascus. According to the dictionary, to *apprehend* means "to capture" or "arrest." God captured Paul's attention. The last thing he wanted to be was a follower of Jesus. He was a declared enemy of Jesus. But God was able to apprehend him anyway.

Don't you worry. God knows exactly how to apprehend your children (and grandchildren!). And when the time comes, He'll do it. After all, you weren't in your prayer closet when He found you!

But, until then, you must stand fast in faith for them. No matter what they get into, no matter how far off the track they seem to be, just keep saying what the Bible says about them. Keep your eyes focused on the covenant mercy of God and not on the symptoms of ungodliness that you see in their lives.

Don't ever give up on your child. If you've grown weak and discouraged lately, it's time for you to get that fire back in your bones. Dig in to the Word of God and dig out the promises He's given you for your children. Lay hold of those promises and don't let go.

Learn to call things that are not as though they were (Romans 4:17). When you hear bad news about your children or you see them do something that hurts your heart, just say: "God, I thank You that Your tender mercy hovers over my child. I thank You, Lord, that he is born again, filled with the Holy Ghost and obedient to You. I thank You that Your Word is in his mouth (Isaiah 59:21), that he is taught by Your Spirit, and great is his peace (Isaiah 54:13). I am not moved by what I feel or what I see. I am moved by Your Word and I call it done in Jesus' Name!"

I'm going to say it one more time: You have a covenant with God that covers your children. So rejoice! God will be faithful to you. One day your boy or your girl will be going about their business doing their own thing when suddenly—*Pssst!*—they'll hear the voice of God.

When that happens, they'll come running. You can count on it.

Evening Reflection

How is it comforting to know that God's mercy hovers over your children?

_____

_____

_____

_____

_____

_____

Zechariah speaks of God "hissing" for your children. What does that mean?

_____
_____
_____
_____
_____
_____

How does God "apprehend" us?

_____
_____
_____
_____
_____

Notes:

_____
_____
_____
_____
_____
_____
_____
_____
_____
_____
_____
_____
_____
_____
_____
_____
_____
_____
_____
_____
_____
_____
_____
_____
_____
_____

Today's Prayer of Faith

Father God, today I stand in the gap for my children. I hold them up before Your throne of grace and thank You that Your mercy hovers over them. I pray that You would soften their hearts and keep them open to the leading of Your Spirit.

Satan, in Jesus' Name, I bind you in your maneuvers against my children. I declare they are disciples taught of the Lord, obedient to His will, and great is their peace and undisturbed composure. In righteousness are they established. They are the fruit of my womb and they are BLESSED!

Real-Life Testimonies
to Help Build Your Faith

Family Reunited

Five years ago my husband and I adopted 6-year-old twins from Russia. We were feeling comfortable and adjusting well with our new children. But, they kept mentioning Kolia and Katya, their older brother and sister still living in Russia. They would cry when they talked about their siblings and missed them very much. We knew in our hearts God wanted us to adopt them too. But how?

We called the adoption agency we had worked with and asked them to find the older siblings. One year later, the agency located Kolia and Katya in an orphanage eight hours from Moscow, but when asked if they wanted to be adopted, they said no. The agency suggested we fly to Moscow. We did and when the four children saw each other they could not stop hugging and kissing. One year after our visit, Kolia and Katya wrote us and asked if we would accept them into our family. Although we were concerned about being able to come up with the money, through the generous financial support of church members, a grant and refinancing our house, we raised enough money within a few months to complete the adoption requirements.

Kolia was 17 and there was a possibility the Russian government would not release him. However, we arrived back in America May 31 with the children. The next day Kolia turned 18 and celebrated his birthday in our home!

S.W.
Delaware

Chapter Nine
Reaching Out to Others

Let the World See Jesus
by Kenneth Copeland

When talking about building relationships that last, it's not long before you realize that God wants us to reach out beyond our family and friends, beyond our comfort zone, and minister to the lost. And people today are hungry to see Jesus.

They don't just want to hear about Him. They don't just want to know what other people say about Him. They want to see Him for themselves. They want to see His character. They want to see His life. They want to see His power.

The time has come for us, as the Body of Christ, to rise up and give them what they want. It's time for us to let Jesus walk and talk and live His life through us. It's time for us, by the power of the Holy Spirit, to do the works that He did so that the world can see Jesus through us.

That's been God's plan for the Church all along. He has always intended for us to reveal Jesus to the world during our earthly lives just as Jesus revealed the Father to the world during His earthly life.

Think about that! Jesus revealed the Father so perfectly that when one of His disciples said, "Lord, show us the Father, and it sufficeth us," Jesus answered him and said, "He that hath seen me hath seen the Father" (John 14:8-9).

What do you think will happen in the world when we manifest Jesus so completely that the same thing can be said of us? What will happen when the people of the world can say of us, "If you've seen them…you've seen Jesus."

I'll tell you what will happen. We'll have a worldwide harvest of souls swept into the kingdom of God the likes of which this earth has never seen!

The Word of God tells us that time is coming. Ephesians 4:13 refers to it as the time when "we all come in the unity of the faith, and of the knowledge of the Son of God, unto a perfect man, unto the measure of the stature of the fulness of Christ."

What's more, the Holy Ghost is letting us know *that time* is *now!* We've entered into the last of the last days. This is the time for the fullness of the manifestation of Jesus through His Body on the earth.

The Excellent Pathway to Power

That's one reason so many Christians desire to operate in the gifts of the Spirit these days. They're responding to the stirring of the Holy Ghost within them. They're sensing the Church shouldn't just be reading about the manifestations of the Spirit described in the New Testament anymore, but rather, Christians should be walking in them!

Many believers today are wholeheartedly obeying the instruction in 1 Corinthians 12:31—they are earnestly coveting spiritual gifts. They long for them. They pray for them. They study the Bible to build faith for them. But for the most part, the Church is still not moving in them fully.

What more can we do?

The Apostle Paul himself answers that question. Right after he tells us to earnestly covet the best gifts he says, "…and yet show I unto you a more excellent way." Then he writes an entire chapter on the subject of *love*.

Pursue love…and desire spiritual gifts (1 Corinthians 14:1). According to the Bible, a more excellent way to walk in the power of God is to pursue love—which is where we started in this LifeLine study, isn't it? That's the best way to develop a lifestyle of doing the works of Jesus. Walking in love is the best way for the world to see Jesus through us.

Why is the way of love such an excellent way? Think about it scripturally for a moment and you'll see the reason. Acts 10:38 tells us that "God anointed Jesus of Nazareth with the Holy Ghost and with power: who went about doing good, and healing all that were oppressed of the devil." So if we're going to do the works Jesus did, we'll do the same thing, right? We'll bring healing and deliverance to those who are oppressed.

Keeping that in mind, consider what Isaiah 54:14 reveals about how the devil inflicts that oppression. It says, "Thou shalt be far from oppression; for thou shalt not fear." According to that scripture, oppression comes from fear! Fear is the spiritual force behind sin, oppression, sickness and every other bondage of the devil. Fear is the spiritual connector to the entire spectrum of death.

But, glory to God, the New Testament tells us that "perfect love casteth out fear" (1 John 4:18). Love destroys the devil's hold. It undermines his whole operation! And not only that, love connects us to the oppression-destroying power of God because that power operates by faith and faith works by love (Galatians 5:6).

The Best Place to Start

How do you grow and develop in love? We studied this a bit in the second session of this book, but it bears repeating: You grow and develop in love the same way you grow and develop in anything else. *You practice it.* You exercise it until you get stronger and stronger in it.

Some people start out by trying to practice love on the meanest, ugliest person they know. But I don't recommend that. The Bible does tell us to love our enemies and to love each other as Jesus loved us. If you start there, however, you're likely to end up frustrated and defeated.

Why is that? Because, according to the Scriptures, the divine cycle of love begins with God's love for us and our love for Him, then it extends outward to other people. The Apostle John said it this way:

> In this was manifested the love of God toward us, because that God sent his only begotten Son into the world, that we might live through him. Herein is love, not that we loved God, but that he loved us, and sent his Son to be the propitiation for our sins. Beloved, if God so loved us, we ought also to love one another.... And we have known and believed the love that God hath to us. God is love; and he that dwelleth in love dwelleth in God, and God in him. Herein is our love made perfect, that we may have boldness in the day of judgment: because as he is, so are we in this world (1 John 4:9-11, 16-17).

According to those verses, the first thing we must do to develop in love is to practice believing the love God has for us. We have to practice believing, for example, what Jesus said in John 17—*that the Father loves us just as much as He loves Jesus!* That's hard to swallow but the Bible says it. So when we find ourselves worrying about something, we should reject fear and practice believing God's love instead.

First the Father—Then the Children

Once you start loving the Lord and receiving His love, you *are* going to love others. It's inevitable! First John 5:1 leaves no doubt about that. It says plainly, "Every one that loveth him that begat loveth him also that is begotten of him." In other words, everyone who loves the Father also loves the children!

We start off loving God because He first loved us. We practice our love on Him and we end up falling in love with everyone around us. As His love begins to flush the fear out of us, suddenly we can drop the barriers that have separated us from other people. We aren't afraid to love them anymore because we know they can't hurt us. We are safe in the love of God.

As a result, we can abandon ourselves to each other. We can forget about our own protection and preservation and just lose ourselves in helping meet the needs of those around us. We can draw on the ministry of Jesus—not just to meet our own needs or to prove we're spiritual hotshots—but because we need His power to take care of others. We need it to help them and heal them and get them free!

It doesn't make any difference how impossible a situation might be, when we have that attitude and that heart of love, the gifts of the Spirit are going to operate. Signs and wonders, healings and miracles are going to break forth. People all over the world—spiritually hungry people—will finally get what they need. They get to see Jesus. They'll see His love. They'll see His life. And they'll see His power.

As we grow up in love, we will walk in the fullness of the measure of the stature of Christ. We will reveal Him just as He revealed the Father...and the world will see Jesus again!

Morning Reflection

How will the world see Jesus in us?

_____

_____

_____

_____

_____

_____

How do the gifts of the Spirit and love work together?

_____

_____

_____

_____

_____

How do you grow and develop in love?

_____

_____

_____

_____

_____

_____

Today's Connection Points

- **Building Relationships That Last CD: "I Can Hear Your Voice" (Track 9)**

    Spend time today listening for the voice of God. He has a plan for every situation you face.

- **DVD: "Represent Jesus in Your Workplace" (Chapter 9)**

    It's time to reach out beyond your comfort zone to let the world see Jesus through you.

- **Love Confessions CD (Track 9)**

    1 Thessalonians 5:8-10; 2 Thessalonians 2:16-17, 3:3, 5; 2 Timothy 1:6-7; Titus 3:4-7, Hebrews 10:24, 13:1, 5-6; 1 John 2:5, 10, 15

Faith in Action

Practice the love of God today.

Believe in His love for you and live faithfully, sharing it with others!

Notes

Without Spot or Wrinkle— The Glorious Church!

by Gloria Copeland

Every generation has had its role in God's ultimate plan for all the earth to be filled with the glory of the Lord (Numbers 14:21).

During the time of Moses, God manifested His power on behalf of the children of Israel in such spectacular ways that they commanded the respect of the Egyptians. When Moses led the Israelites out of bondage, they were truly regarded as God's people because of the unquestionable demonstration of His supernatural power.

In the same way, the day has come for God to raise up the Body of Christ—the glorious Church—without spot or wrinkle. This Church will command the respect of the world because it has the miraculous power of God in manifestation with signs and wonders! The Church will show forth the glory of God.

But first, God's people must become faithful and available to God—like Moses was. God needed Moses' obedience because Moses' job was to stretch out his hand in the earth and command the will of God to be done. God had to have someone who would dare to act on His Word. When Moses stretched out his hand, God extended *His* hand and performed miracles, signs and wonders!

God was able to use Moses because Moses knew His ways (Psalm 103:7). If Moses had not been faithful to know God's ways, the children of Israel would never have seen His acts.

Today the Spirit of God is dealing with us much in the same way as He dealt with Moses. We have experienced a move in the Body of Christ in which God has taught us His ways. We have learned to live according to the Word. We have been taught to walk by faith and not by sight because God needs people with a solid foundation in His Word.

God needs faithful, obedient people in this hour because He is going to once again show Himself strong in the earth. He needs those who have made His Word the final authority in their lives. Those who know how to depend on God's Word will be the backbone of this move of the Spirit.

Practice Faithfulness

As we fine-tune our lives to obey the promptings of the Holy Spirit, God will have available the vessels necessary to manifest Himself in the earth. The key element is this: God is not looking for *ability*. He is looking for *availability*.

God's plan is for this generation to sweep the souls of this earth into the kingdom of God. But to do this, supernatural power will be required just as it was required to deliver the children of Israel! The Spirit of God, through the Body of Christ, will deliver the children of men from the power of darkness by the power of the Holy Spirit.

Do you see why, when God called Moses, He chose a man who would be obedient? Moses had what it took to accomplish the great feat of delivering Israel: He was faithful. Faithfulness results in action. That is called obedience!

If God is to use us as He used Moses, we must be faithful, too. We have learned to practice faith. But God wants us to learn to practice faithfulness to fulfill all that He has planned.

God Wants Your Heart!

Far too often men and women have heard the word of faith and have tried to walk in the integrity of God's Word without putting their hearts into it. They want the good things—health, prosperity, victory and blessed relationships—without giving themselves to God and serving Him with their whole hearts.

Jesus said, "This people draweth nigh unto me with their mouth, and honoureth me with their lips; but their heart is far from me" (Matthew 15:8). In other words, we can confess the Word of God from now until Jesus comes, but if our hearts are not right, it will not come to pass.

Until we get our priorities right, the things of this world will continue to steal time and energy from us that we should be giving to the things of the spirit. We will be so caught up in using our faith for the affairs of this world that our desire will be for the things of the world instead of for God.

Too many have tried to have the best of both worlds—prospering financially but not dedicating to the ways of God (which in reality is the way to prosper). They may experience some outward success that way, but they will not experience the blessings and power of God to the degree He desires for them. Money without peace will only increase the problem.

Much Given, Much Required

God requires more of us because we have revelation knowledge of His Word. "For unto whomsoever much is given, of him shall be much required" (Luke 12:48).

We are a generation to whom much has been given. God has not trained us in His Word so we can consume it on our own lusts. He has revealed His Word to us so we would walk in the spirit while we live in a natural, physical world.

We must walk in the spirit to fulfill God's plan for this hour. We must let go of our allegiance to this natural world and put God first place in our lives. Jesus said, "For whosoever will save his life shall lose it; but whosoever shall lose his life for my sake and the gospel's, the same shall save it" (Mark 8:35).

We have a job to do. God needs us to reach the ends of the earth with the gospel. We are the carriers of His Word. We are the Word made flesh, just as Jesus was. We have the same opportunity Jesus had to do the will of the Father. He laid down His life in glory to come to the earth and make a way for us to be born again.

Jesus came to set up His kingdom, and He did. We enter into that kingdom by grace through faith. We are messengers of God's grace, telling the world they can be born again by faith in Jesus Christ.

The Faithful Are Blessed

When Jesus ascended into heaven, He gave us His Name, His authority and His power. He said to preach the gospel to every creature, cast out devils and lay hands on the sick. He gave us our assignments and sent the Holy Spirit to endue us with the power necessary to fulfill those assignments (Mark 16:15-20; Matthew 28:19-20; Acts 1:8, 2:1-4).

In Matthew 28, Jesus told the disciples to teach the converts to "observe all things whatsoever I have commanded you" (verse 20). The Body of Christ is to carry on exactly as Jesus did.

You can look at Church history and see the talents the Master has given each generation. He has brought one revival after another, waiting for the Church to do what He commanded. Now we are entering into the revival of the glory of God and of the Spirit being manifest to all flesh. Jesus is giving this generation the responsibility of walking in the spirit so the glory of God will be revealed in us.

Whether you received five talents or two, God expects you to be faithful now (Matthew 25:14-30). He wants you to grow right where you are and become faithful over what He has assigned you to do. Prove yourself faithful over little, and God will make you ruler over much.

We need to tell God every day, "Lord, You can count on me. I love You, and I am here to serve You. I deny my own interests. I lay aside the pleasures of this life, and I make myself available to You today. What do You want me to do?"

As we come to that place spiritually, we will begin to walk in an area with God we thought would be possible only in heaven!

Are You Available?

How will we be able to walk in the spirit even though we are clothed with this flesh? By spending more time pursuing the things of the spirit than we spend pursuing the things of the flesh.

We will have to become dedicated to prayer and fellowship with God. We must be dedicated to the Word of God and be willing to pull aside from this busy life around us to get alone with God so He can guide us, teach us and communicate with us.

Our natural ability does not determine our usefulness. All we have to be are those who live in the presence of God. He has the ability!

We make ourselves available to Him by praying in the spirit, worshiping and fellowshiping with Him. He can then manifest His character, His nature, His glory and His Spirit in us. That is what He wants to do. He came to live inside us so He could radiate from the inside out! That's what happened with Jesus.

When Jesus was on the Mount of Transfiguration, the glory of God within Him radiated outward, and He was transfigured. "His face did shine as the sun, and his raiment was white as the light" (Matthew 17:2).

And since God is the same yesterday, today and forever, it will happen the same way in our day. God has never changed His ways. The glory of God will come from inside us—from our inner man—as we give ourselves totally to Him and walk in the spirit.

We were predestined to be conformed to the image of Jesus (Romans 8:29-30). God has reproduced Himself through believers—the Church—so He can show Himself to the world.

Now it's time for the glorious Church to shine!

Evening Reflection

How does God want to use His people in these last days?

_____
_____
_____
_____
_____
_____

How will walking in the spirit bring God's glory into the earth?

_____
_____
_____
_____
_____
_____

Why is *availability* more important than *ability* to God?

_____
_____
_____
_____
_____
_____

Notes

_____
_____
_____
_____
_____
_____
_____
_____
_____
_____
_____

_____
_____
_____
_____
_____
_____
_____
_____
_____
_____
_____
_____
_____
_____
_____
_____
_____
_____
_____
_____
_____
_____
_____
_____
_____
_____
_____
_____

Today's
Prayer of Faith

Father God, I am a vessel, available to You. Mold me and use me for Your glory, so that everyone I come in contact with will experience You and Your love in me. Open my eyes to opportunities to reach out to the lost as a member of the Body of Christ. I am available!

Gift of Salvation Blesses Family

In 2003, just after my wife and I were married, we were praying for our families' salvation. The Lord showed me a vision of a pebble being dropped into something that looked like a still lake. The pebble caused ripples to form and the Lord spoke and said, *Your prayers have caused ripples in the spirit realm and your families will be saved.*

A year later we received another word from the Lord that, "Out of our mouths a trumpet will sound and bring our families into the kingdom." That put a spring in our step and we continued praying for our families until March 2008. I was watching the New Year's Eve service where Brother Copeland ministered at EMIC. Near the end of the service he said something that grabbed my attention. He said, "Stop worrying about your kinfolk, stop wrestling with it, stop your work and enter into His finished work." Then he gave an example of prayer that should be said concerning families.

The next day I got out my prayer diary, wrote down that prayer, brought it before God, declared it and entered His rest regarding their salvation. Two days later my wife's aunts and grandmother came to our house. They all had complaints about various illnesses and knew of my faith in believing for healing, prosperity, guidance and trusting in what the Lord has said in His Word. The Holy Spirit told me to read Mark 2 where Jesus heals the paralytic through the faith of his friends. I told them that just as the paralytic's friends had used their faith, I was going to use mine and they would have to take immediate action and believe they were healed—regardless of what their bodies might say through pain, etc. I also said that receiving their healing but still ending up in hell would be a shame and they should think about their eternal salvation.

As I was praying the Lord said to me, *Ask them if they want to be saved,* so I asked if anyone wanted to give Jesus a chance and invite Him into their lives. One by one they raised their hands and were led from the kingdom of darkness into the kingdom of light! I'm resting in God's finished work and my whole family is saved. Jesus Is Lord!

J.H.
United Kingdom

Chapter Ten
Serving Jesus Together

We Need Each Other
by Kenneth Copeland

A LifeLine book on "Building Relationships That Last" would be incomplete without a look at the power of *partnership*. This is a facet of relationships that is especially close to my heart, since it has completely transformed our lives and ministry. For that reason, I'm going to take both the morning and evening connection today to talk about partnership. I believe you will be blessed for it!

My friend, if ever there were a generation that needed to live and walk in faith and love, it's the generation in which you and I now live. Thank God we have His Word and His powerful Anointing. But also, thank God we have each other. We need each other! We need each other's faith. We need each other's prayers.

In these days especially, it is important that we partner with anointed, praying people because—as we are about to see—our individual anointings and prayers of faith flowing together in one direction are far more powerful than any one of us alone could ever be.

Gloria and I are privileged and honored to have more than 200,000 anointed, praying and believing Partners around the world who have joined their faith and love with Kenneth Copeland Ministries. These are believers who are committed to support KCM in every way that the Spirit of God leads them.

I don't mind telling you that it's a great source of joy and strength just knowing that there are so many Partners out there standing strong with us, wherever we might be in the world, facing whatever storms we might have to face. After all, it takes far more than what Gloria and I have in order to get the message of victory in Jesus into the hands of God's people. It takes partnership!

For more than 40 years of ministry, we have been like the Apostle Paul who, when he wrote to his partners, said:

I thank my God in all my remembrance of you. In every prayer of mine I always make my entreaty and petition for you all with joy (delight). [I thank my God] for your fellowship—your sympathetic cooperation and contributions and partnership—in advancing the good news (the Gospel) from the first day [you heard it] until now (Philippians 1:3-5, *The Amplified Bible).*

Sure, the list of KCM Partners is long. And it's getting even longer since the Spirit of God told Gloria and me that we will have 1 million Partners—*and we will!* But that list of names, however long it may be, is not set up to be some tool for us to use when we decide to mail something.

No, that list of names represents real, flesh-and-blood, Holy Ghost-anointed people who are in covenant with us—and with each other—helping us serve the God of covenant. Gloria and I hold these precious souls in our hearts every moment of every day. Not a day goes by that we don't pray for our Partners, using a list of specific scriptures that the Lord has given us to pray, *and believe,* on their behalf.

Spiritual Principles

You see, when Paul wrote this letter to his partners in Philippi, he wasn't just scratching out some nice words to make them feel good about themselves. No, he was explaining some very important spiritual principles where ministry was concerned. He was explaining the exchange, or two-way flow, of God's grace and power in partnerships established for the purpose of ministry.

Certainly, prayer is a major part of this partnership exchange, and it is the focus of our study. But Paul was saying that there was even more being transferred in the exchange:

Being confident of this very thing, that he which hath begun a good work in you will perform it until the day of Jesus Christ: Even as it is meet for me to think this of you all, because I have you in my heart; inasmuch as both in my bonds, and in the defence and confirmation of the gospel, ye all are partakers of my grace (Philippians 1:6-7).

Basically, Paul was telling his partners, "Hey, we're in this together. And the grace—or anointings—that God put on me, He has put on you by having joined us together. So expect every anointing and blessing that I have operating in my life to operate in yours, too!"

Think of the more than 200,000 Partners and the KCM staff around the world who are praying—all of us agreeing and joining our faith together.

I guarantee you that partnership—corporate prayers, corporate anointings, corporate faith—will turn a bad situation around!

Where covenant partnership is concerned, it is important for us to understand that when you pray for me, you're praying for Gloria. When you pray for Gloria, you're praying for me. When you pray for us, you're praying for a Partner in Texas, and others around the world, too. And when Gloria and I pray for them, we're praying for you.

Do you see the exchange and flow of prayer and anointing? Do you see the strength of it?

That's how God designed it. That's what partnership is all about. It's about partaking of each other's grace.

To his partners, Paul stated:

For I know that this shall turn to my salvation through your prayer, and the supply of the Spirit of Jesus Christ [the Anointed One], according to my earnest expectation and my hope, that in nothing I shall be ashamed, but that with all boldness, as always, so now also Christ [the Anointed One and His Anointing] shall be magnified in my body, whether it be by life, or by death (Philippians 1:19-20).

Here, it's obvious that Paul earnestly expected his partners to pray and stand with him so he could do what he had been called by God to do. He expected his partners to covenant with him, to join with him and undergird him with prayer.

It was those prayers that were vital to Paul's ministry because they were his connection to an even greater supply of the Spirit—a greater supply of anointing which was necessary to get the job done. The prayers of all those believers—Paul's partners—were his connection to their corporate anointings.

No Spectators Here!

In all my years as a believer and as a minister of the gospel, I have observed how the Church has had a tendency to stand back and let the anointed ministers of God bear most of the responsibility in carrying out the commandments of Jesus. Too often we've sat back like an audience or room full of spectators, and watched as the pastors, evangelists, and so on, did the work.

My brother and sister, that has never been God's intention.

When Jesus of Nazareth was baptized in the waters of the Jordan River, in that moment the Spirit of the Lord came on Him and baptized Him for public ministry (John 1:29-34; Luke 4:18-19).

Jesus walked this earth bearing all the Anointings of God, being the fullness of God manifest in the flesh. Yet, when He went up from the banks of the Jordan and began His earthly ministry, He chose 12 partners with whom to get started.

Let's take that a step further: Not only did Jesus need their partnership, He also needed their prayers. In Matthew 26 and Mark 14, Jesus went to the garden in Gethsemane, along with His disciples—His partners—to pray.

In perhaps His greatest hour of need, Jesus looked to His partners for their support. He needed their presence and their prayers. Three different times during that spiritual night watch, He indicated that He needed their help. As it turned out, it was also one of the disciples' greatest hours of need, but they gave in to their flesh. They slept.

Today is no different. You and I are in the middle of a night watch, waiting for the return of Jesus, and the Church is in perhaps its greatest hour of need.

If Jesus and the Apostle Paul needed the prayers and support of their partners, Gloria and I certainly need the prayers and support of our Partners to complete what God has called us to do. And you need partnership to do what God has called you to do, too.

My friend, the Bible says one of us can put a thousand to flight, and two of us 10,000 to flight (Deuteronomy 32:30). Just imagine what more than 200,000 Partners—joined together over the miles—are doing right at this moment.

Better yet, imagine what *1 million* will do!

Morning  Reflection

What is partnership?

How does partnership bless everyone who is partnered?

Whom can you join in partnership today to ensure your—and their—success?

Today's Connection Points

- ### *Building Relationships That Last* CD: "Body of Christ" (Track 10)

  As you listen to this track, meditate on how you can be more like Jesus and touch the world around you with His love.

- ### DVD: "Partnership: Together We Are Making A Difference" (Chapter 10)

  When we follow the leadership of the Holy Spirit, and come together in partnership as He directs, we'll all be fully supplied. None of us will lack anything.

- ### *Love Confessions* CD (Track 10)

  1 John 3:1, 11, 14-16, 23, 4:7-21, 5:1-5; 2 John 5-6; Jude 20-21; Revelation 1:5-6

Pray for those with whom you are in partnership today.
If you're not in a partnership covenant, take time to seek the Lord about the ministries with whom He would have you partner.

Notes

_____

_____

_____

_____

_____

_____

_____

_____

_____

_____

_____

_____

_____

_____

_____

_____

_____

_____

_____

_____

_____

_____

_____

_____

_____

_____

_____

_____

_____

_____

_____

_____

The Prophet's Reward
by Kenneth Copeland

Before we finish this study together, I want to take a closer look at the "partnership exchange" we briefly talked about in the last session. This is so important because it is an absolute key to your success in every area of life—from finances to health, from enhancing your spiritual growth to helping you build relationships that last.

Partnership is literally a spiritual gold mine. It is a mine so deep, so rich, you will never be able to plumb the depths of it in this lifetime. Obviously, I can only scratch the surface of it here. But if you'll spend some time on your own studying what God's Word says about it, you'll realize, as I have, that the power of partnership is greater than anything you've ever imagined.

Let's look in the Word and you will see that—contrary to what many people have thought—partnership is not a new idea some fundraiser cooked up. It is an ordinance of God that began in the Old Testament and continued in the New. It is a system designed by God to dramatically increase the abilities, resources and rewards of every believer.

Establishing Partnership

That system was officially established and recognized as an ordinance of God in 1 Samuel 30. There we find David and the men who fought under his command in hot pursuit of the Amalekites who had plundered their homes and taken their families captive.

In order to overtake their enemy, David's men had embarked on a grueling military maneuver known as a "forced march." That's a march under pressure which involves moving the most men and equipment as far and as fast as possible, while remaining battle ready at all times. It's a tough assignment, and by the time David's men reached the brook Besor, 200 of them were too exhausted to go on.

David instructed the weary ones to remain behind and guard the supplies. Then he and the rest of the men went on across, found the Amalekites, and—by the power of God—jerked the slack out of them! They not only defeated the army and recovered all their own possessions, but they also took what belonged to the Amalekites. So when they came back across the Besor, they brought with them great spoil!

When the fighting men rejoined the 200 others, however, some of them didn't want to share the rewards of that war with those who had stayed behind. "Because they went not with us, we will not give them aught of the spoil that we have recovered," they said (verse 22).

It was at that moment that David, a man after God's own heart, officially established the principle of partnership. He said:

> My brethren, you shall not do so with what the Lord has given us, who has preserved us and delivered into our hand the troop that came against us. For who will heed you in this matter? But as his part is who goes down to the battle, so shall his part be who stays by the supplies; they shall share alike." So it was, from that day forward; he made it a statute and an ordinance for Israel to this day (1 Samuel 30:23-25, *New King James Version*).

On the Front Lines Together

You may think that ordinance doesn't mean much for you. But it does. After all, you're a soldier just like David's men were. You are a part of the army of Jesus, the Anointed One. You're on a mission to occupy this earth and enforce the devil's defeat until Jesus returns.

You may not be on the front lines of the fivefold ministry. You may not hold the office of an apostle, prophet, evangelist, pastor or teacher. But if you're in partnership with a minister who is doing the work of God, fighting alongside him or her through prayer or through giving, you'll receive an eternal reward for every person who is born again, and every believer who is strengthened, healed or delivered as a result of that minister's endeavors.

If, for example, a million people make Jesus the Lord of their lives through the outreaches of Kenneth Copeland Ministries this year, God gives you, as a Partner, credit for every one of them. Why is that? It's because, just like the soldiers who stayed and guarded the stuff, you did your part. You prayed. You gave. You helped us by joining your faith with ours.

So as far as God is concerned, you deserve to be rewarded just as much as Gloria and I do because your part is just as important as ours!

"Well, I'd like to believe that, Brother Copeland, but that was an Old Testament ordinance. Are you sure it's still in effect today?"

Yes! Jesus taught the first 12 disciples about it. He reaffirmed to them that principle of partnership by saying:

> He that receiveth a prophet in the name of a prophet shall receive a prophet's reward; and he that receiveth a righteous man in the name of a righteous man shall receive a righteous man's reward. And whosoever shall give to drink unto one of these little ones a cup of cold water only in the name of a disciple, verily I say unto you, he shall in no wise lose his reward (Matthew 10:41-42).

An Earthly Reward

It would be sufficiently exciting if the reward we received from our partnership in God's work were strictly a heavenly reward. But praise God, it's not!

There's also an earthly aspect to this reward system. Partnership is one of God's ways of providing for us, here and now, blessings so great we could never muster up enough faith to receive them on our own.

You can see what I mean if you'll read 2 Kings 4:8. There you'll find the account of a Shunammite woman who decided to support the ministry of the prophet Elisha. She was so determined to be a partner in his work that one day when he was passing by she "constrained him to eat bread." She just wouldn't take no for an answer. She insisted that he stay for dinner.

She didn't stop with that, either. She and her husband built a special room on to their house so Elisha would have a place to stay whenever he was in town.

Do you know what Elisha did in return? He called in his servant, Gehazi, and said, "Go find out what I can do for this woman. Find out what she desires."

So Gehazi went, checked out the situation, then came back and told Elisha:

> Verily she hath no child, and her husband is old. And [Elisha] said, Call her. And when he had called her, she stood in the door. And he said, About this season, according to the time of life, thou shalt embrace a son. And she said, Nay, my lord, thou man of God, do not lie unto thine handmaid (verses 14-16).

Obviously, this woman didn't have the faith to believe God for a child because when Elisha told her she would bear a son, she said, "No way! You may be a prophet, but you're lying to me now!" That was out there beyond what she could ask or think.

But Elisha didn't have any trouble believing for it, and since she was due a reward and they were in partnership with one another, he just released his faith on her behalf. Sure enough, by the next year that Shunammite woman had a baby.

Take Advantage of the Privileges

That same principle will operate for you today just like it did for her. If you're a Partner with Gloria and me, for example, you've joined up with our faith. Now when we started out, we just had enough faith to keep our old car running so we could get from one meeting to the next. But over the years, as this ministry has grown, we've learned how to believe for the millions of dollars it takes to pay television bills and salaries, buy equipment and such.

If you're newer to this faith life than we are, or if you haven't had the opportunities to grow in it that we have, you may have some needs that are out beyond your faith range right now. For example, you might have $50,000 worth of debt you'd like to pay. You know God *can* do it, but at this point in your life, it may be hard for you to believe He *will* do it for you.

Well, take advantage of the privileges of partnership. Believing for $50,000 worth of debt reduction isn't hard for Gloria and me.

As I said, we have to believe for millions every month. So write that $50,000 debt-reduction prayer request on the sheet I send you every month with my letter, and send it back. Use it as a way to release your faith in the God-ordained power of partnership.

Of course, that applies to believing for relationships, too. You may be believing for the salvation of a family member or a child to come back home. You may be praying for a stronger marriage or great favor with your employer. Whatever relationship you are dealing with, believe me: In over 40 years of ministry, we've faced it! Let this book be simply the starting point for your restoration—and don't go it alone. Write down that need, and allow us to join in faith with you for it.

That's why I provide that sheet. I don't do it just because it's the traditional thing to do. I'm energizing you to take part in the prophet's reward! We have a prayer staff that prays over those requests. Plus, Gloria and I pray every day for our Partners just like we pray for our own family. We're exercising our faith on your behalf, so reach out and receive some of the blessings you have coming to you!

Increase Your Anointing

Realize those blessings aren't limited to this natural, material realm. Through partnership, the *anointings* God has given Gloria and me for ministry are also available to you.

The Apostle Paul understood that principle. That's why in the letter to his Philippian partners he had the boldness to say:

> I thank my God upon every remembrance of you, always in every prayer of mine for you all making request with joy, for your fellowship [or partnership] in the gospel from the first day until now; being confident of this very thing, that he which hath begun a good work in you will perform it until the day of Jesus Christ: Even as it is meet for me to think this of you all, because I have you in my heart; inasmuch as both in my bonds, and in the defence and confirmation of the gospel, ye all are partakers of my grace (Philippians 1:3-7).

We touched on this in the last session, but let's look even closer. Look at that last phrase: "ye all are *partakers of my grace.*" Not God's grace. *My* grace! In other words, Paul was saying, "As my partners, you share in the grace God has given me to carry out my ministry."

If you'd like to see how significant that really is, just read through some of Paul's letters and see the statements he makes about grace. Statements such as, "By the grace of God I am what I am...I laboured more abundantly than they all: yet not I, but the grace of God which was with me" (1 Corinthians 15:10).

Paul was literally telling the Philippians that as his partners, the same anointings that were on him as an apostle had become available to them!

I don't know about you, but I desire all the anointing I can get. That's why I partner with the ministries of Oral Roberts, Kenneth Hagin, Jerry Savelle, Jesse Duplantis, Creflo Dollar and many others—to be a partaker of their grace!

"But I don't need those kinds of anointings!" you may say. "I'm not a preacher. I'm just a mechanic...or a housewife...or a salesman."

That may be your profession, but aren't you called to witness to people, pray for them and minister to them as you go about your daily affairs? Of course you are! And the more of the Anointing of God you have available to you, the better you'll be able to do it.

What's more, when you partner up with a ministry, whatever anointing is on you—the mechanic anointing, the real estate anointing, etc.—becomes available to that ministry. When you understand that, you can see as we follow the leadership of the Holy Spirit and come together in partnership as He directs, we'll all be fully supplied. None of us will lack anything.

Spiritually, we'll have the full scope of the Anointing of God. And materially we'll enjoy the prophet's reward. By joining in faith together, we receive exceeding, abundantly above what we can ask or think!

I'm convinced it was that reward Paul had in mind when, in closing his partner letter to the Philippians, he told them, "My God shall supply all your need according to his riches in glory by Christ Jesus" (Philippians 4:19)!

No matter how you look at it, that deal is just too good to pass up. So don't! Make up your mind right now to seek God and find out with whom He'd have you become a partner. Then be like that Shunammite woman and start looking for ways to bless your partner.

You'll have so much fun at it, you'll be tempted to forget all about the reward. But God won't. If you'll stay connected in faith, He'll see to it that you're blessed with more of everything than you ever dreamed possible. He'll see to it that you receive the prophet's reward.

What is the principle of partnership that David established after defeating the Amalekites?

_____
_____
_____
_____
_____
_____

How does partnership contain both spiritual and earthly rewards?

_____
_____
_____
_____
_____
_____

What are you believing God for as you join a ministry in partnership?

_____
_____
_____
_____
_____
_____

Notes

_____
_____
_____
_____
_____
_____
_____
_____
_____
_____
_____
_____
_____

_____
_____
_____
_____
_____
_____
_____
_____
_____
_____
_____

Today's
Prayer of Faith

*Father, I stand in faith for those with whom I'm in partner-
ship. Bless them beyond measure, minister strength and
healing to them, and supply all their needs. Thank You that
the anointing and grace that is on their ministries is on my
life and ministry, too—for we strengthen and encourage one
another! I believe we receive and are heirs together of the
grace of life.*

Real-Life Testimonies
to Help Build Your Faith

No Longer Alone

I'm feeling so much better, and oppression has lifted since becoming a Partner
with KCM. I listen to Ken pray for me and all his Partners on CD while making
my coffee in the morning. *I no longer feel alone in my walk with the Lord.* I also
pray each day for the ministry and Partners and spend more time in the Word
and in prayer and watching the messages I've been sent. I'm encouraged to go
on and *my hope is restored.* Thank you for being there for me and for letting me
know I'm not alone.

F.S.
Canada

In what three areas has your faith grown the most from your use of *all* the LifeLine materials?

1. _____

   _____

2. _____

   _____

3. _____

   _____

List three ways you are putting your faith into action right now.

1. _____

   _____

2. _____

   _____

3. _____

   _____

As your faith has grown, what are three ways you can be a blessing to others this week?

1. _____

   _____

2. _____

   _____

3. _____

   _____

Appendix A
Prayers and Confessions
Based on God's Word

These can also be found on your Faith in Action Cards.

James 4:8
I draw near to God today...and He draws near to me!

1 John 4:12
I love others and God dwells in me! His love is perfected—made complete—in me.

1 Corinthians 13:5
I do not insist on my own rights or my own way. I am not self-seeking. I am not touchy, fretful or resentful. I take no account of evil done to me nor pay attention to suffered wrongs. I choose to live a life of forgiveness—a life of BLESSING!

2 Timothy 2:21
I cleanse myself of dishonor. I declare I am a vessel of honor, sanctified and useful for the Master, prepared for every good work.

Romans 12:10; Ephesians 6:2-3
As a member of the Body of Christ, I am devoted to my brothers and sisters in the Lord. I honor others above myself. And because I honor my father and mother, it will go well with me, and I will live long on the earth.

Ephesians 4:29
I let no unwholesome talk come out of my mouth—but only that which is helpful for building others up, that it may minister grace to the hearers.

Genesis 18:19
I direct my children to keep the way of the Lord and I live uprightly before them, doing what is right and just, and the Lord will bring about what He has promised me!

Isaiah 54:13; Zechariah 10:8
My children are taught of the Lord and their peace is great. The Lord signals for them, gathers them in and redeems them.

1 Corinthians 14:1
I live a life in pursuit of love and I desire spiritual gifts. Others see God's love in me!

Matthew 10:41
I receive a prophet because he is a prophet—in partnership with him—and I receive a prophet's reward!

Appendix B
Relationship Promises

It's God's desire that your relationships be blessed—from the relationships in your household to the relationships in your workplace and church. In addition to the prayers and confessions on your Faith in Action Cards, here are more promises you can study and stand on as you believe God for the absolute *best* in all your relationships!

Promises for Your Household

Deuteronomy 26:11
And thou shalt rejoice in every good thing which the Lord thy God hath given unto thee, and unto thine house.

Deuteronomy 28:8
The Lord shall command the blessing upon thee in thy storehouses, and in all that thou settest thine hand unto; and he shall bless thee in the land which the Lord thy God giveth thee.

Joshua 24:15
But as for me and my house, we will serve the Lord.

Psalm 91:10
There shall no evil befall thee, neither shall any plague come nigh thy dwelling.

Proverbs 3:33
The curse of the Lord is in and on the house of the wicked, but He declares blessed (joyful and favored with blessings) the home of the just and consistently righteous. *(The Amplified Bible)*

Proverbs 12:7
The wicked are overthrown, and are not: but the house of the righteous shall stand.

Proverbs 15:6
In the house of the righteous is much treasure: but in the revenues of the wicked is trouble.

Acts 16:31
Believe on the Lord Jesus Christ, and thou shalt be saved, and thy house.

Promises for Your Marriage

Song of Solomon 7:10
I am my beloved's, and his desire is toward me.

Song of Solomon 8:7
Many waters cannot quench love, neither can the floods drown it.

Mark 10:9
What therefore God hath joined together, let not man put asunder.

1 Corinthians 11:3
But I would have you know, that the head of every man is Christ; and the head of the woman is the man; and the head of Christ is God.

Ephesians 4:32
And be ye kind one to another, tenderhearted, forgiving one another, even as God for Christ's sake hath forgiven you.

Ephesians 5:21
Submitting yourselves one to another in the fear of God.

Hebrews 13:4
Let marriage be held in honor (esteemed worthy, precious, [that is,] of great price, and especially dear) in all things. And thus let the marriage bed be undefiled (kept undishonored). *(The Amplified Bible)*

1 Peter 3:8-9
Finally, all [of you] should be of one and the same mind (united in spirit), sympathizing [with one another], loving [each the other] as brethren [of one household], compassionate and courteous (tenderhearted and humble). Never return evil for evil or insult for insult (scolding, tongue-lashing, berating), but on the contrary blessing [praying for their welfare, happiness and protection, and truly pitying and loving them]. For know that to this you have been called, that you may yourselves inherit a blessing [from God—that you may obtain a blessing as heirs, bringing welfare and happiness and protection]. *(The Amplified Bible)*

Promises for Husbands and Fathers

Proverbs 5:18-19
Let thy fountain be blessed: and rejoice with the wife of thy youth. Let her be as the loving hind and pleasant roe; let her breasts satisfy thee at all times; and be thou ravished always with her love.

Proverbs 18:22
Whoso findeth a wife findeth a good thing, and obtaineth favour of the Lord.

1 Corinthians 7:3

The husband should give to his wife her conjugal rights (goodwill, kindness, and what is due her as his wife), and likewise the wife to her husband. *(The Amplified Bible)*

Ephesians 5:25-33

Husbands, love your wives, even as Christ also loved the church, and gave himself for it; that he might sanctify and cleanse it with the washing of water by the word, that he might present it to himself a glorious church, not having spot, or wrinkle, or any such thing; but that it should be holy and without blemish. So ought men to love their wives as their own bodies. He that loveth his wife loveth himself. For no man ever yet hated his own flesh; but nourisheth and cherisheth it, even as the Lord the church: For we are members of his body, of his flesh, and of his bones. For this cause shall a man leave his father and mother, and shall be joined unto his wife, and they two shall be one flesh. This is a great mystery: but I speak concerning Christ and the church. Nevertheless let every one of you in particular so love his wife even as himself; and the wife see that she reverence her husband.

Colossians 3:19

Husbands, love your wives and do not be bitter toward them. *(New King James Version)*

1 Peter 3:7

Likewise, ye husbands, dwell with [your wives] according to knowledge, giving honour unto the wife, as unto the weaker vessel, and as being heirs together of the grace of life; that your prayers be not hindered.

Proverbs 19:14

House and riches are the inheritance of fathers: and a prudent wife is from the Lord.

1 Timothy 3:4

He must rule his own household well, keeping his children under control, with true dignity, commanding their respect in every way and keeping them respectful. *(The Amplified Bible)*

Promises for Wives and Mothers

Proverbs 11:16

A gracious woman retaineth honour: and strong men retain riches.

Proverbs 12:4

A virtuous woman is a crown to her husband: but she that maketh ashamed is as rottenness in his bones.

Proverbs 14:1

Every wise woman buildeth her house: but the foolish plucketh it down with her hands.

Proverbs 31:10-31

Who can find a virtuous woman? for her price is far above rubies. The heart of her husband doth safely trust in her, so that he shall have no need of spoil. She will do him good and not evil all the days of her life. She seeketh wool, and flax, and worketh willingly with her hands. She is like the merchants' ships; she bringeth her food from afar. She riseth also while it is yet night, and giveth meat to her household, and a portion to her maidens. She considereth a field, and buyeth it: with the fruit of her hands she planteth a vineyard. She girdeth her loins with strength, and strengtheneth her arms. She perceiveth that her merchandise is good: her candle goeth not out by night. She layeth her hands to the spindle, and her hands hold the distaff. She stretcheth out her hand to the poor; yea, she reacheth forth her hands to the needy. She is not afraid of the snow for her household: for all her household are clothed with scarlet. She maketh herself coverings of tapestry; her clothing is silk and purple. Her husband is known in the gates, when he sitteth among the elders of the land. She maketh fine linen, and selleth it; and delivereth girdles unto the merchant. Strength and honour are her clothing; and she shall rejoice in time to come. She openeth her mouth with wisdom; and in her tongue is the law of kindness. She looketh well to the ways of her household, and eateth not the bread of idleness. Her children arise up, and call her blessed; her husband also, and he praiseth her. Many daughters have done virtuously, but thou excellest them all. Favour is deceitful, and beauty is vain: but a woman that feareth the Lord, she shall be praised. Give her of the fruit of her hands; and let her own works praise her in the gates.

Ephesians 5:22-24

Wives, submit yourselves unto your own husbands, as unto the Lord. For the husband is the head of the wife, even as Christ is the head of the church: and he is the saviour of the body. Therefore as the church is subject unto Christ, so let the wives be to their own husbands in every thing.

Ephesians 5:33

The wife see that she reverence her husband.

Colossians 3:18

Wives, submit yourselves unto your own husbands, as it is fit in the Lord.

Titus 2:3-5

The aged women likewise, that they be in behaviour as becometh holiness, not false accusers, not given to much wine, teachers of good things; that they may teach the young women to be sober, to love their husbands, to love their children, to be discreet, chaste, keepers at home, good, obedient to their own husbands, that the word of God be not blasphemed.

Psalm 113:9

He maketh the barren woman to keep house, and to be a joyful mother of children.

Promises for Your Children

Proverbs 6:20-22

My son, keep thy father's commandment, and forsake not the law of thy mother: Bind them continually upon thine heart, and tie them about thy neck. When thou goest, it shall lead thee; when thou sleepest, it shall keep thee; and when thou awakest, it shall talk with thee.

Proverbs 13:1

A wise son heareth his father's instruction.

Matthew 18:10

Take heed that ye despise not one of these little ones; for I say unto you, That in heaven their angels do always behold the face of my Father which is in heaven.

Luke 2:40

And the Child grew and became strong in spirit, filled with wisdom; and the grace (favor and spiritual blessing) of God was upon Him. *(The Amplified Bible)*

Ephesians 6:1-3

Children, obey your parents in the Lord: for this is right. Honour thy father and mother; which is the first commandment with promise; that it may be well with thee, and thou mayest live long on the earth.

1 Timothy 4:12

Let no one despise or think less of you because of your youth, but be an example (pattern) for the believers in speech, in conduct, in love, in faith, and in purity. *(The Amplified Bible)*

2 Timothy 2:22

Flee also youthful lusts: but follow righteousness, faith, charity, peace, with them that call on the Lord out of a pure heart.

Promises for Singles

Psalm 68:6

God places the solitary in families and gives the desolate a home in which to dwell. *(The Amplified Bible)*

Proverbs 15:25

The Lord will destroy the house of the proud: but he will establish the border of the widow.

Isaiah 54:5

For thy Maker is thine husband; the Lord of hosts is his name; and thy Redeemer the Holy One of Israel; The God of the whole earth shall he be called.

Jeremiah 29:11

For I know the thoughts that I think toward you, saith the Lord, thoughts of peace, and not of evil, to give you an expected end.

1 Corinthians 7:32, 34

My desire is to have you free from all anxiety and distressing care. The unmarried man is anxious about the things of the Lord—how he may please the Lord.... And the unmarried woman or girl is concerned and anxious about the matters of the Lord, how to be wholly separated and set apart in body and spirit. *(The Amplified Bible)*

James 1:27

Pure religion and undefiled before God and the Father is this, To visit the fatherless and widows in their affliction, and to keep himself unspotted from the world.

Promises for Your Brothers and Sisters in Christ

Psalm 133:1

Behold, how good and how pleasant it is for brethren to dwell together in unity!

Proverbs 17:17

A friend loveth at all times, and a brother is born for adversity.

Ecclesiastes 4:9-12

Two are better than one; because they have a good reward for their labour. For if they fall, the one will lift up his fellow: but woe to him that is alone when he falleth; for he hath not another to help him up. Again, if two lie together, then they have heat: but how can one be warm alone? And if one prevail against him, two shall withstand him; and a threefold cord is not quickly broken.

Matthew 18:18-20

Verily I say unto you, Whatsoever ye shall bind on earth shall be bound in heaven: and whatsoever ye shall loose on earth shall be loosed in heaven. Again I say unto you, That if two of you shall agree on earth as touching any thing that they shall ask, it shall be done for them of my Father which is in heaven. For where two or three are gathered together in my name, there am I in the midst of them.

John 13:34

A new commandment I give unto you, That ye love one another; as I have loved you, that ye also love one another.

Romans 12:10

Be kindly affectioned one to another with brotherly love; in honour preferring one another.

Galatians 3:28-29

There is neither Jew nor Greek, there is neither bond nor free, there is neither male nor female: for ye are all one in Christ Jesus. And if ye be Christ's, then are ye Abraham's seed, and heirs according to the promise.

Galatians 6:1-2

Brethren, if a man be overtaken in a fault, ye which are spiritual, restore such an one in the spirit of meekness; considering thyself, lest thou also be tempted. Bear ye one another's burdens, and so fulfil the law of Christ.

Galatians 6:10

As we have therefore opportunity, let us do good unto all men, especially unto them who are of the household of faith.

1 John 1:7

But if we walk in the light, as he is in the light, we have fellowship one with another, and the blood of Jesus Christ his Son cleanseth us from all sin.

1 John 4:7

Beloved, let us love one another; for love is [springs] from God; and he who loves [his fellowmen] is begotten (born) of God and is coming (progressively) to know and understand God [to perceive and recognize and get a better and clearer knowledge of Him]. *(The Amplified Bible)*

Appendix C

Relationship Prayers and Confessions

Prayer for Your Marriage

Father, it is written in Your Word that we are to esteem our marriage as precious, of great price and especially dear. We agree with Your Word and act accordingly.

By a conscious act of our wills, we put away strife by becoming swift to hear, slow to speak and slow to anger. We confess and believe that we neither offend nor take offense with one another.

Your Word says You have knit us together in purpose and power, therefore we commit ourselves and our marriage to be the mighty instrument on earth that You designed us to be. Our desire is to be an example of Your love to our family, friends and all with whom we come in contact.

So Father, right now, we make a quality decision to live in unity and harmony. We agree not to give ourselves over to selfish desires that cause division and distrust. We declare that we honor and value our union by keeping our marriage bed undefiled. We declare that our marriage grows stronger every day and is an encouragement to those around us. We will conduct ourselves honorably and becomingly—being kind, tenderhearted, compassionate, understanding and loving toward one another. We are always ready to believe the best, and freely forgive one another.

Father, we declare and therefore it is established that we live in a peaceable habitation and quiet resting place. Thank You, Lord, for making us heirs together of the grace of life! We make this commitment before Your throne in the Name of Jesus and by the authority of Your Word. Amen.

References from T*he Amplified Bible:* Hebrews 13:4; 2 Timothy 2:24-26; Colossians 1:10; Philippians 2:2, 4:7; Ephesians 4:32; Isaiah 32:17-18; Jeremiah 1:12; James 1:19, 3:2; 1 Peter 3:7; Mark 11:23; Matthew 18:19; Philippians 2:3

Prayer for Your Children

In the Name of Jesus, I believe in my heart and therefore say with my mouth that the Word of God prevails over my children. Your Word says You will pour out Your Spirit upon my offspring and Your blessing upon my descendants. So I declare by faith that my children hear the voice of Your Spirit and the voice of strangers they will not follow. Thank You that my children are wise, take heed to and are the fruit of godly instruction and correction. I love the children You have blessed me with and I diligently discipline them early. Because of that, they give me delight and rest.

Father, You said You will contend with him who contends with me, and You give safety to my children and ease them day by day. I receive that promise by faith and declare that my children are blessed when they come in and when they go out. Thank You for giving Your angels special charge over my children to accompany and defend and preserve them. I believe they find favor, good understanding and high esteem in Your sight, Lord, and in the sight of man.

I confess that my children are disciples taught of the Lord and obedient to Your will. Great is their peace and undisturbed composure. I believe I receive wisdom and counsel in bringing them up in the discipline and instruction of the Lord. And Your Word declares that when they are old they will not depart from it. So I commit them to Your keeping and have confident trust that You watch over and bless them all the days of their lives. In Jesus' Name. Amen.

References from *The Amplified Bible:* Mark 11:23; Isaiah 44:3; Proverbs 13:1, 24, 29:17; Isaiah 49:25; Deuteronomy 28:6; Psalm 91:11-12; Proverbs 3:4; Isaiah 54:13; Proverbs 2:6; Ephesians 6:4; Proverbs 22:6

Confession for Your Marriage

I declare by faith that my marriage is blessed. My spouse and I are heirs together of the grace of life and we are led by the Spirit of God. When we pray together in unity, our prayers are powerful and get results. Peace and harmony reign in our home. We walk in agreement and are an unstoppable force for God's kingdom. My spouse and I stand together in united spirit and purpose, with single minds in faith, proclaiming the glad tidings of the gospel.

Strife has no dominion in our relationship. If we become angry, we are quick to forgive. We are not self-seeking, rude, proud, boastful or jealous. Instead, we are loving, kind, patient and put each other's needs before our own. We trust each other and protect the sanctity of our marriage. God joined us together as one, and we will not be separated.

References: Deuteronomy 28:1-14; Romans 8:14; Philippians 1:27 *(The Amplified Bible);* Matthew 18:19; 1 Peter 3:7; Mark 11:25; Romans 13:13; 1 Corinthians 13:4-8; Matthew 19:6

Confession for Your Children

God's mercy hovers over my children. The covenant I have with God in the blood of Jesus extends to my children (and grandchildren)—covering them completely. Everything God gives me, He gives my children. I call them disciples, taught of the Lord. Great is their peace and undisturbed composure. I speak the protection of the Lord over my children according to Psalm 91 and declare that no evil befalls them, neither does any plague or calamity come near them. I lay hold of God's plans and purposes for my children by faith, and I call those things to come to pass in their lives. Because their steps are ordered by the Lord, I say by faith they are always in the right place, at the right time, doing the right things. God's perfect will is being done in their lives.

I believe and trust in God for my children's (and grandchildren's) guidance and salvation. The Lord strengthens and completes them, making them what they ought to be and equips them with everything good so that they may carry out His will. I roll the care of them over on the Lord and put all my trust in Him concerning them. I am filled with joy because I know they are turning to the Lord, and I am sure that He who began a good work in them will continue it until the day of Jesus Christ, perfecting and bringing that good work to full completion in them. I'm not moved by what I see or hear, but only by what the Word says. My children follow after Him and press toward the mark for the prize of the high calling of God in Jesus. I believe that He captures their hearts, and they love and serve Him all the days of their lives.

References: Psalm 103:7; Romans 4:17; Zechariah 10:7-9; Isaiah 54:13; Psalm 91, 37:23; Hebrews 13:21 *(The Amplified Bible);* Matthew 6:10; 1 Peter 5:7; Philippians 1:6 *(The Amplified Bible);* Proverbs 22:6; Philippians 3:12, 14

Confession for All Your Relationships

I enjoy sharing random acts of kindness. When I see people in need, I feel compassion toward them. I am not rude, proud or self-seeking. When people hurt me, I am quick to forgive. I walk in harmony and peace with family, friends and co-workers.

I have good relationships with others because God's love in me flows toward them. I put others' needs before my own. My heart is gentle, and I am patient with others as I lift them up in times of need. Because of God's love for me and in me, I excel in the grace of giving.

References: John 15:12; Matthew 6:14; 1 Corinthians 13; Psalm 133:1; Romans 12:10; Ephesians 4:2; Hebrews 10:24; 1 Peter 3:8; 2 Corinthians 8:7

Additional Materials to Help You
Build Relationships That Last

Books

- A Ceremony of Marriage
- Blessed to Be a Blessing
- Be a Vessel of Honor
- Family Promises
- God's Success Formula
- God's Will for You
- Love—The Secret to Your Success
- One Word From God Can Change Your Family
- One Word From God Can Change Your Relationships
- Raising Children Without Fear
- The Winning Attitude
- Turn Your Hurts Into Harvests
- To Know Him
- Walk With God

Audio Resources

- A Lifestyle of Love
- Becoming a Woman of God
- Developing Friendship with God
- Enemies of Love
- God's Plan for Man
- Living in the Blessing (8-CD series)
- Love Confessions
- Love—Your First Priority
- The Kingdom of God—Days of Heaven on Earth (5-CD series)
- Six Steps to Excellence in Ministry

Video Resources

- Finding True Love God's Way
- Kingdom Principles
- Living in the Blessing (2-DVD set)
- The Blessing: The Power, the Purpose and the Manifestation (2-DVD set)

Prayer for Salvation and Baptism in the Holy Spirit

Heavenly Father, I come to You in the Name of Jesus. Your Word says, "Whosoever shall call on the name of the Lord shall be saved" (Acts 2:21). I am calling on You. I pray and ask Jesus to come into my heart and be Lord over my life according to Romans 10:9-10: "If thou shalt confess with thy mouth the Lord Jesus, and shalt believe in thine heart that God hath raised him from the dead, thou shalt be saved. For with the heart man believeth unto righteousness; and with the mouth confession is made unto salvation." I do that now. I confess that Jesus is Lord, and I believe in my heart that God raised Him from the dead.

I am now reborn! I am a Christian—a child of Almighty God! I am saved! You also said in Your Word, "If ye then, being evil, know how to give good gifts unto your children: HOW MUCH MORE shall your heavenly Father give the Holy Spirit to them that ask him?" (Luke 11:13). I'm also asking You to fill me with the Holy Spirit. Holy Spirit, rise up within me as I praise God. I fully expect to speak with other tongues as You give me the utterance (Acts 2:4). In Jesus' Name. Amen!

Begin to praise God for filling you with the Holy Spirit. Speak those words and syllables you receive—not in your own language, but the language given to you by the Holy Spirit. You have to use your own voice. God will not force you to speak. Don't be concerned with how it sounds. It is a heavenly language!

Continue with the blessing God has given you and pray in the spirit every day.

You are a born-again, Spirit-filled believer. You'll never be the same!

Find a good church that boldly preaches God's Word and obeys it. Become part of a church family who will love and care for you as you love and care for them.

We need to be connected to each other. It increases our strength in God. It's God's plan for us.

Make it a habit to watch the *Believer's Voice of Victory* television broadcast and become a doer of the Word, who is blessed in his doing (James 1:22-25).

About the Authors

Kenneth and Gloria Copeland are the best-selling authors of more than 60 books. They have also co-authored numerous books including *Family Promises* and *From Faith to Faith—A Daily Guide to Victory*. As founders of Kenneth Copeland Ministries in Fort Worth, Texas, Kenneth and Gloria are in their 42nd year of circling the globe with the uncompromised Word of God, preaching and teaching a lifestyle of victory for every Christian.

Their daily and Sunday *Believer's Voice of Victory* television broadcasts now air on more than 500 stations around the world, and their *Believer's Voice of Victory* magazine is distributed to more than 1 million believers worldwide. Their international prison ministry reaches an average of 60,000 new inmates every year and receives more than 17,000 pieces of correspondence each month. Their teaching materials can also be found on the World Wide Web. With offices and staff in the United States, Canada, England, Australia, South Africa and Ukraine, Kenneth and Gloria's teaching materials—books, magazines, audios and videos—have been translated into at least 22 languages to reach the world with the love of God.

Learn more about Kenneth Copeland Ministries
by visiting our Web site at **www.kcm.org**

World Offices
Kenneth Copeland Ministries

For more information about KCM and our products,
please write to the office nearest you:

Kenneth Copeland Ministries
Fort Worth, TX 76192-0001

Kenneth Copeland
Locked Bag 2600
Mansfield Delivery Centre
QUEENSLAND 4122
AUSTRALIA

Kenneth Copeland
Private Bag X 909
FONTAINEBLEAU
2032
REPUBLIC OF
SOUTH AFRICA

Kenneth Copeland Ministries
Post Office Box 84
L'VIV 79000
UKRAINE

Kenneth Copeland
Post Office Box 15
BATH
BA1 3XN
U.K.

Kenneth Copeland
PO Box 3111 STN LCD 1
Langley BC V3A 4R3
CANADA

We're Here for You!

Believer's Voice of Victory Television Broadcast

Join Kenneth and Gloria Copeland and the *Believer's Voice of Victory* broadcasts Monday through Friday and on Sunday each week, and learn how faith in God's Word can take your life from ordinary to extraordinary. This teaching from God's Word is designed to get you where you want to be—*on top!*

You can catch the *Believer's Voice of Victory* broadcast on your local, cable or satellite channels.* Also available 24 hours on webcast at BVOV.TV.

> * Check your local listings for times and stations in your area.

Believer's Voice of Victory Magazine

Enjoy inspired teaching and encouragement from Kenneth and Gloria Copeland and guest ministers each month in the *Believer's Voice of Victory* magazine. Also included are real-life testimonies of God's miraculous power and divine intervention in the lives of people just like you!

It's more than just a magazine—it's a ministry.

To receive a FREE subscription to
Believer's Voice of Victory, write to:

Kenneth Copeland Ministries
Fort Worth, TX 76192-0001
Or call:
800-600-7395
(7 a.m.-5 p.m. CT)
Or visit our Web site at:
www.kcm.org

If you are writing from outside the U.S., please contact the KCM office nearest you. Addresses for all Kenneth Copeland Ministries offices are listed on the previous pages.